Profiles from History

Heroes of America's Growth and Freedom

- Volume 2 -

Ashley M. Wiggers

Profiles from History - Volume 2
Copyright © 2010 Ashley M. Wiggers

Portrait illustrations © 2010 Cheryl Ellicott
Map illustrations by Kathy Wright

ISBN: 978-1-931397-64-3
Library of Congress Control Number: 2010916510

Published by Geography Matters, Inc.
800.426.4650
www.geomatters.com

Printed in the United States of America

Dedication

To the great men and women of this country's history, thank you for your inspiration.

To my husband and my parents, your love and support made this possible.

Table of Contents

Instructions

In *Profiles from History - Volume 2*, I tried to take a unique perspective on each historical figure by sharing some of the lesser known facts that you may not have learned before. For instance, when learning about Joshua Chamberlain and Stonewall Jackson, I didn't focus merely on their achievements in battle, but more on their strength of character. As you read each profile it is my hope that you will connect with the person, not just the history.

In this book you will read about authors, scientists, statesmen, and everyday people that made a significant difference in the world around them and forever changed the future. Beginning around 1770 and continuing through 1930, the exploits of many famous people are described with an eye to seeing their motivations and the impact their lives had on others.

Use *Profiles from History* either to enhance lessons in history and social studies or as a stand-alone book. Choose the fun projects in this book according to the interests of each student. Select as many or as few of the activities as you would like. Each profile can be used as a read-aloud, or your student can use the story for independent reading. To get the full benefit from each profile, I recommend students use several of the following activities provided to tap into the different approaches taken:

Discussion questions: inspire critical thinking and help the student relate to each historical figure.

Follow-up activities: relate to the accomplishments of each profile, connecting the child by hearing, seeing, and doing to the importance of each person's story.

Word games: such as word searches and crossword puzzles focus on key words to remember from the profile while increasing comprehension and vocabulary.

Critical thinking activities: include sequencing of events and determining the meaning of words using context.

Maps: help students visually pinpoint either the location where the historical figure came from, or the area in which the main event of their life took place.

Timelines: give the student an overview of the time period in which the historical figure lived and connect each person with other important events occurring at the same time. A reference timeline is included with each profile. Students are instructed to place timeline figures on a timeline. This timeline and the figures are located in the back of the book before the answer keys.

Also Available

Profiles from History - Volume 2 activities and reproducibles in digital format for your convenience.

If you enjoy the format and focus of this book you may be interested in *Profiles from History - Volume 1*. This book includes profiles of men and women that greatly influenced the exploration and founding of our country in the time period of 1200 - 1890.

Patrick Henry

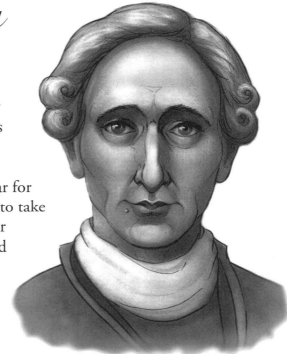

An orator, by definition, is "a public speaker, especially one who is eloquent or skilled." Patrick Henry is known for being one of the most famous orators of the American Revolution. He was such a fearless and gifted speaker that when our country was on the verge of a war for independence, he gave people the courage to take that step toward freedom. It was in the year 1775 when he gave his most passionate and famous speech. It was so empowering that afterward the crowd is said to have jumped up and yelled, "To arms! To arms!"

These were some of his words:

> *"Is life so dear, or peace so sweet, as to be purchased at the price of chains and slavery? Forbid it, Almighty God! I know not what course others may take; but as for me, give me liberty, or give me death!"*

Patrick had an average upbringing, raised by loving parents in a typical home along with his brothers and sisters. He tried his hand at several different professions as a young man. But it wasn't until he was twenty-four years old that he found his true calling—the study and practice of law. Becoming a lawyer set the stage for his immense role in America's fight for independence.

Typically, when a person wanted to become a lawyer in the late 1700s he would either be apprenticed under someone with experience, or he would study law in England. Patrick Henry decided to take the third, more difficult option of teaching himself. Virginia, where he lived, required that those wanting to become lawyers must appear before a board of examiners who were appointed by a general court.

One of the obstacles Patrick had to overcome in his life was that he was poor as a young man. He dressed in plain clothes and was very much an outdoorsman. He loved to hunt and fish, and simply enjoyed being outside. When he first came before the law examination board in Williamsburg, the men were reluctant to see him because of the way he looked. Undoubtedly they wondered if this country boy was intelligent enough for such a prestigious position. It must have taken great courage for him to stand before those wealthy and well-educated men.

Needless to say, they did see him and were astonished by his knowledge and strength of speech. He received his license to practice law. However, this young man's law career did not really begin until a few years later with a case called the Parson's Cause. After winning this case, Patrick Henry became a household name and was widely revered as the people's champion.

The Parsons Cause came about when the colonists passed an act that restricted the amount of payment a clergymen (or parson) from the Anglican Church would receive. Since the clergy were considered servants of the state, their salaries were to be paid through the taxation of the people. The restriction on their payment was necessary because times were hard, and crops were not yielding good enough harvests for the town to be able to pay the wages. Some clergymen decided to sue in order to get their full salaries.

Henry fought for the people who would have to pay the clergy, namely the farmers and the townspeople, who had precious little to spare. He argued that the clergyman wanted to take money away from the very people he was supposed to be helping. Patrick Henry didn't start his speech with the confidence and stature for which he would later be known. But as he spoke, he began to stand a little straighter and speak with a little more authority. By the end of his speech the crowd and the jury were whole-heartedly behind him. They awarded the clergyman one penny in damages, and Patrick Henry became a hero. One account states that the people lifted Henry up on their shoulders after the jury had spoken, and Henry's father, who was the presiding judge in the case, was moved to tears.

After his fame spread, Henry was asked to fill a vacancy in the House of Burgesses. The Virginia House of Burgesses consisted of a group of men (representatives from different counties and cities) who were a kind of legislature. Amidst such leaders as

Thomas Jefferson and George Washington, it took Henry only nine days to make his presence known. The Stamp Act had just been permitted by the King and declared that a tax be paid on every single piece of paper used by the colonists. The House of Burgesses had not approved this act. A distant and tyrannical government that did not seem to have their best interests in mind was forcing it on them. So Patrick Henry submitted resolutions that opposed the Stamp Act. These resolutions would be the first actions in the revolution.

Loved and respected by the people Henry served in many different ways, During the Revolutionary War he led the militia which was entrusted with Virginia's safe-keeping. He served as a member of the Continental Congress. He became Virginia's first governor, under the new Constitution, and ultimately served five terms. One of our esteemed Founding Fathers, Patrick Henry served this country with a kind of determination and fervor that may have been unmatched. He earned the admiration and respect of some of the most remarkable leaders this country has ever seen. It is with great gratitude and humility that we remember this hero of our past, who fought desperately for our future.

Discussion

Reread the excerpt of Patrick Henry's speech in paragraph 2. In your own words, retell what Henry said. Do you think he was willing to take this course of action even if no one else did? Is there anything that you believe in that you would be willing to speak boldly about, even if no one else agreed with you? Tell your parent or teacher about it. Have you ever spoken up about something and been the only person who felt that way? How did you feel? Did other people oppose or disagree with you? Did it make it hard to continue in your beliefs? Compare your feelings to those of Patrick Henry. Does this make his speaking out even more impressive to you?

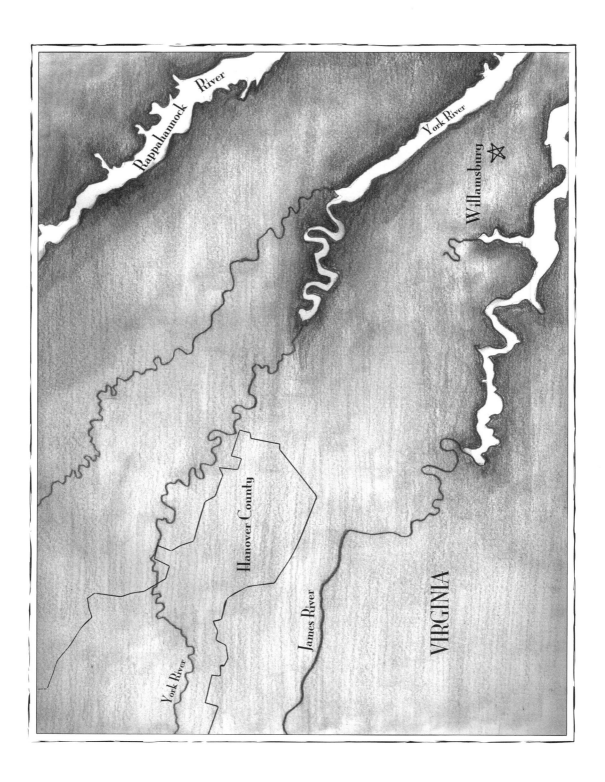

Timeline Review

Put things in perspective. Place Patrick Henry's figure on the timeline in the year 1775, which was when he made his most famous speech. Look at the other events before, during, and after this year.

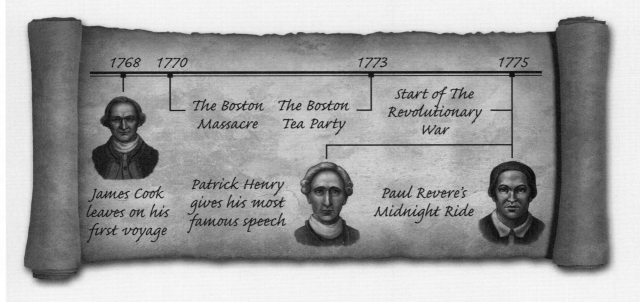

Activity

You are going to consider two positions and make a list of points that support each one. After you have done this, which position was easier to support? Why do you think so?

> Position 1: My country is the best country in the world.
> Position 2: My country is not the best country in the world.

How do you think this activity relates to the study of Patrick Henry? Do you think he would have been able to equally support both positions? Why or why not?

Wordscramble

Here is a list of scrambled words that relate to the profile you read about Patrick Henry. Unscramble the letters and write the words correctly.

1. ratHyPenikrc _____
2. srasoeauCnPs _____
3. tarroo _____
4. aamsntest _____
5. ylewar _____
6. iiVinagr _____
7. tamSpctA _____
8. odsotuonmra _____
9. ephcse _____
10. naopsr _____

Before and After

Read the event on the left side and the event on the right side. Then decide if the first event (on the left) happened **before** or **after** the second event (on the right). Choose the word in the middle column that is correct. You may circle the correct answer or draw a line from the words *before* or *after* to the matching event.

1	Patrick Henry gave his famous "Give me liberty, or give me death!" speech.	Before	After	The Revolutionary War began.
2	Henry was asked to fill a vacancy in the House of Burgesses.	Before	After	Patrick Henry earned his license to practice law.
3	The Revolutionary War began.	Before	After	Henry submitted resolutions opposing the Stamp Act.
4	Henry argued the case called the Parson's Cause.	Before	After	Henry led the Virginia militia during the Revolutionary War.
5	Henry was elected Governor of Virginia.	Before	After	Henry was a member of the Continental Congress.

Patrick Henry Word Search

```
X B I T G K E S B V C J T Y S L D C J
N E Z B E C H T G O R K U B B A H U W
D O R A T O R A R U B O C W W W A Z P
G Z T R I Y S T A K O Z C T N Y Q Q A
Y H Q I H D X E B K O M H H Y E T J T
F Q A P K Y Q S W S H K Z G W R B T R
G Y O S P K J M O U S T A M P A C T I
H C S P C V I A L N P H C D I J G U C
Q S T E N G P N P A R S O N W U K S K
J Z Q E Y W O U T D O O R S M A N G H
D E F C G P R I C H N G I Q N G P Z E
F L C H Y T R X O T F B E F W A S Z N
A P A R S O N S C A U S E K X S P U R
W C E M A B Q A H R V I R G I N I A Y
O A Q H D P Q Q P K P O Z L U E O G A
```

Word Bank

lawyer

orator

outdoorsman

parson

Parson's Cause

Patrick Henry

speech

Stamp Act

statesman

Virginia

Patrick Henry Crossword

Across

1. a clergyman in the Anglican church
3. one of the original thirteen colonies that became a state
4. someone skilled in speaking
5. a tax requiring payment for any paper used in the colonies
6. a talk given before an audience
7. someone who is qualified to give legal advice and representation
8. a widely respected senior politician

Down

1. lawyer, statesman, and orator from Virginia
2. a case that challenged an English tax
4. someone who spends much time in outdoor activities

Paul Revere

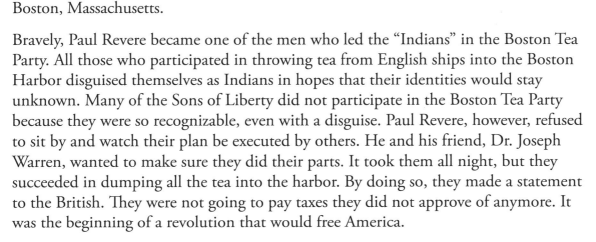

They met in a secret place, swore silence to one another, and spoke of things considered treason—treason in the eyes of England that is! It was the year 1773, and the air was thick with restlessness. The British were doing all they could to hold on to control of America. They patrolled the streets and monitored the people. They forced the colonists to pay them tax upon tax of their hard earned money. As a result, a secret society was formed; a society of men who were referred to as the Sons of Liberty. They are now known as the heroes of our nation. Among these patriots was a man named Paul Revere, a very talented silversmith from the city of Boston, Massachusetts.

Bravely, Paul Revere became one of the men who led the "Indians" in the Boston Tea Party. All those who participated in throwing tea from English ships into the Boston Harbor disguised themselves as Indians in hopes that their identities would stay unknown. Many of the Sons of Liberty did not participate in the Boston Tea Party because they were so recognizable, even with a disguise. Paul Revere, however, refused to sit by and watch their plan be executed by others. He and his friend, Dr. Joseph Warren, wanted to make sure they did their parts. It took them all night, but they succeeded in dumping all the tea into the harbor. By doing so, they made a statement to the British. They were not going to pay taxes they did not approve of anymore. It was the beginning of a revolution that would free America.

After everyone else who had joined in the act went to bed, that's when Paul moved to his next job. He got on his horse and rode all the way to Pennsylvania and New York to spread the news about what they had done. His goal was to inspire other patriots, and to let them know the Sons of Liberty backed up what they said they stood for with their actions.

Many leaders of the revolution were distinguished members of society. One of Revere's important contributions was that he created a bridge between those leaders and the ones who were less wealthy and refined. He was a silversmith, and even though his friends were among the distinguished, he wasn't. He represented the men whose hard work and bravery made just as much of an impact as anyone's.

After the Boston Tea Party, things only grew more and more tense. The more England tried to gain control of America, the more they seemed to lose. On the evening of April 18, 1775, Paul Revere set out on a journey that would place him in America's history books forever. That night the British secretly made the first move of the Revolutionary War, but the Sons of Liberty had been keeping watch and were ready for them. One of their spies sent word that the British troops were on the move, and it was suddenly time for Paul Revere to put his plan into action.

In preparation for this day he had a boat waiting to take him across the Charles River, and had already set up a quick warning system for the town that was just on the other side of the river, Charlestown. It was to be one lantern in the Old North Church steeple if the British were coming by land, and two if by sea. After Paul saw the signal, he borrowed a horse and rode as fast as he could into the night. William Dawes was also assigned the job of warning the patriots, except he was sent the long way around to Lexington just in case Revere was caught. Fortunately, Paul made it to his destination safely, but not without trouble. He ran into two English officers on his way. They did their best to stop him, but fortunately he outran them. He risked his life to fulfill this imperative duty. Finally, after alerting each house along the countryside that the soldiers were coming their way, Revere made it to Lexington. He found John Hancock and Samuel Adams and let them know that the British were marching to arrest them.

Countless lives were saved because of Paul Revere's bravery and quick actions. Without him, America might have lost two of the most important members of the revolution before the war even began—Hancock and Adams! Not to mention the fact that his warning gave colonial militias time to hide the supplies and weapons they had been stockpiling. I wonder if he knew at the time how important his actions were. Did he ever imagine that someday most Americans would know his name and what it represents? I bet if we were able to talk to him he would simply say, "I was just doing my job." That's what this country was built on. Men who risked their lives for the betterment of us all and who would, if given the chance, do it all over again without regret.

"A hurry of hoofs in a village street,
A shape in the moonlight, a bulk in the dark,
And beneath, from the pebbles, in passing, a spark
Struck out by a steed flying fearless and fleet;
That was all! And yet, through the gloom and the light,
The fate of a nation was riding that night;"

– from "Paul Revere's Ride" by Henry Wadsworth Longfellow

Discussion

The men who led the fight against the British, known as the American Revolution, were men who were respected leaders in the community. They were soldiers, lawyers, craftsmen, and government officials. Many were pastors. War was certainly not their first choice as a course of action. Everything else that they knew to do had failed. When they chose this course of action, it was at the risk of their lives, the lives of their families, their homes, jobs, and all that they had. Do you think war was an easy decision for them? Why or why not? Do you think that going to war has ever been an easy decision for leaders to make? What do you think would cause you to agree with war as a solution to a situation?

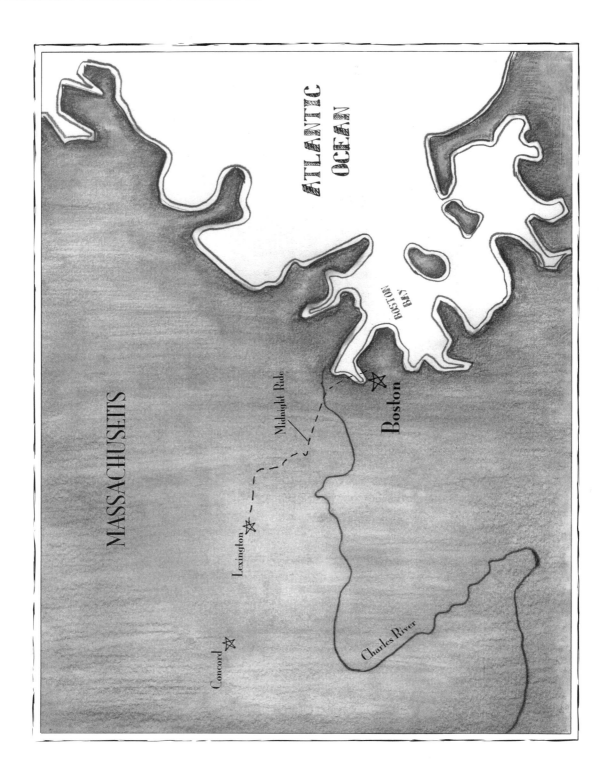

Timeline Review

Put things in perspective. Place Paul Revere's figure on the timeline in the year 1775, which was when he made his famous Midnight Ride. Look at the other events before, during, and after this year.

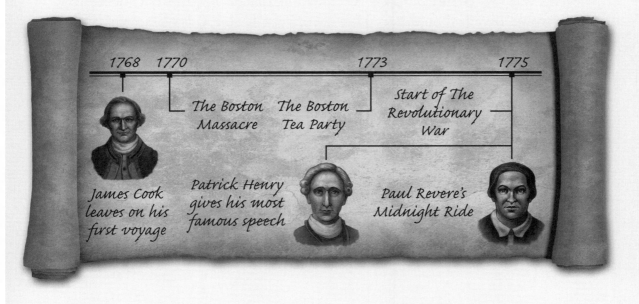

Activity

Read the full poem entitled Paul Revere's Ride by Henry Wadsworth Longfellow. As often happens with literature, the author adds his imaginations of what took place along with the facts. While this poem may not be entirely factual in nature, retelling the events was not its only purpose. After reading this poem, tell what affect you think it would have had on others. How would you have felt, if you were a patriot or supporter of the American Revolution? How would you have felt if you had not been a supporter of the Revolution? You may want to present this poem to your family, class, or group by reading it dramatically, or with expression in your voice, as if you are telling the story from your own personal experience.

Wordscramble

Here is a list of scrambled words that relate to the profile you read about Paul Revere. Unscramble the letters and write the words correctly.

1. trnaeso _____

2. nyoofsieSbtLr _____

3. otaritsp _____

4. mhistlsrvie _____

5. tdehndiiMgRi _____

6. tnanlre _____

7. ieoLtgnxn _____

8. litrueoovn _____

9. ePRvrelaeu _____

10. eevtiripam _____

Using Context

Read the sentence and then look at the word in *italics*. Tell what you think that word means. Then look it up in a dictionary to confirm, or make sure of, the meaning. Tell someone about each word that you got correct. Remember, you will get better at understanding word meanings as you practice using context, or the words around a word.

1. They met in a secret place, swore silence to one another, and spoke of things considered *treason*—treason in the eyes of England that is! (paragraph 1)

   I think *treason* means: _____

   Dictionary definition: _____

   My meaning was: (Circle one)　　　correct　　　had correct parts　　　not close

2. His goal was to inspire other *patriots*, and to let them know the Sons of Liberty backed up what they said they stood for with their actions. (paragraph 3)

   I think *patriots* means: _____

   Dictionary definition: _____

   My meaning was: (Circle one)　　　correct　　　had correct parts　　　not close

3. He risked his life to fulfill this *imperative* duty. (paragraph 6)

   I think *imperative* means: _____

   Dictionary definition: _____

   My meaning was: (Circle one)　　　correct　　　had correct parts　　　not close

Paul Revere Word Search

```
Q P S J O E S N I Z V T R E A S O N N
H D L O B T Q Z K P A J F R K P L G T
L T E T E F P E Z W G B U M Z T R O R
T U X S I L V E R S M I T H T F N S W
P X I R I C P B M G V G C O E Q T W V
L H N E M V C P A T R I O T S O I K K
N Z G V P A U L R E V E R E M N C Q R
E H T O E U K Q G L S T D O H A B W J
C F O L R M E F T A K C D G W A R R J
C J N U A P M I D N I G H T R I D E K
Q Z E T T H U S V T I Z Z K R N K K E
X G C I I G N P L E P V P N C R U X A
A P N O V A I L C R P P F V V G I H G
M A T N E U K Q Q N R N A I G W G U E
Z C A S O N S O F L I B E R T Y X I I
```

Word Bank

imperative
lantern
Lexington
Midnight Ride
patriots

Paul Revere
revolution
silversmith
Sons of Liberty
treason

Paul Revere Crossword

Across

2. the Massachusetts location of Samuel Adams and John Hancock

4. the means used to signal Paul Revere from a church steeple

7. something that is absolutely necessary

9. betraying your country by word or deed

10. a group of citizens devoted to obtaining liberty for America

Down

1. the dramatic change or overthrow of a government, or political system

3. Paul Revere's historic ride to alert colonists to British attack

5. someone who is skilled in making or repairing silver objects

6. a patriotic silversmith from Boston

8. people who proudly support or defend their country

Thomas Paine

*"For all men being originally equals,
no one by birth could have a right
to set up his own family in perpetual
preference to all others forever"*

-Thomas Paine, *Common Sense*

Something that we take for granted nowadays is the right to vote. All United States citizens have an equal right to cast one vote each and elect the officials that govern them. Not so long ago people in this country were forced to abide by rules and pay dues to a distant king whose only qualification as a leader was the family he was born into. People had no say or choice in the laws that were passed down to them. There are still countries today that live under such tyranny. America, however, is no longer one of them. It is thanks to a handful of brave men who stood up and refused to follow unjust rules. They knew that a united people, fighting for something worth fighting for, could prevail against an army of men whose hearts did not belong to a cause, or to a king, but only to self-preservation.

Among the brave men who stood against such tyranny was Thomas Paine. With eloquence he enlightened the people of this soon-to-be-great nation. Being an Englishman, he knew from personal experience when he told Americans that their only chance of happiness was through independence.

He wrote a pamphlet that became a best seller not only in America, but in Europe as well. This pamphlet was accurately named *Common Sense*. It changed the united colonies forever. For possibly the first time, ordinary people could grasp the outrageous idea that there was a better way. There was a way by which each person could be considered equal and worthy of input. Up until this point, America was not wholly convinced that separation from the motherland was the best option. However, after reading Paine's inspiring and illuminating words, many had no choice but to see the truth. Some might say he contributed greatly to our freedom.

Thomas Paine had a rare gift. He could inspire people with just his words. He could explain the complicated theories that drove him in simple, easy-to-understand ways. He did this several times throughout his life. The first time was in England when he was fighting for his and his coworker's rights. The next time was only a couple years after Paine moved to the New World and was the pamphlet called *Common Sense*. After that, he wrote a pamphlet that George Washington read to his troops during the Revolutionary War. Washington used it to motivate his men, to help them remember why they were fighting, and to let them know that they would never be forgotten by the country that owed them so much. This pamphlet was called *The Crisis*. Here are its opening lines:

> *"THESE are the times that try men's souls. The summer soldier and the sunshine patriot will, in this crisis, shrink from the service of their country; but he that stands by it now, deserves the love and thanks of man and woman."*

The Crisis was either read by, or read to, most every soldier in the war at the time. No doubt it did just what it was intended to do—inspire, encourage, and remind each soldier of just how much they were appreciated.

> *"Let it be told to the future world, that in the depth of winter, when nothing but hope and virtue could survive, that the city and the country, alarmed at one common danger, came forth to meet and to repulse it."*

-Thomas Paine

Thomas Paine never stopped to consider the consequences of following what he believed. He just knew that no matter what happened, he must stand for what he felt was right. If something was worth his time, he fully devoted himself to it. Because of this fearless quality he ended up being thrown out of England after writing *The Rights of Man*, and later was imprisoned in France for opposing the execution of King Louis

XVI. Thankfully, with help from the Unites States minister to France, James Monroe, Paine only had to endure one year of prison. About ten years later he received an invitation from Thomas Jefferson to return to America. So, in his sixties Thomas Paine came back to the country to which he had given so much.

It was only seven years later that he stopped fighting altogether. Unfortunately, his last major work was an attack on Christianity and the Bible, even though he believed that equality and liberty were parts of our God-given nature. He made many enemies through this work and spent his last years as an outcast. Sadly, because of his views on religion and his abrasively intense personality, Thomas Paine died in poverty and without recognition.

> *"I love the man that can smile in trouble, that can gather strength from distress, and grow brave by reflection. 'Tis the business of little minds to shrink; but he whose heart is firm, and whose conscience approves his conduct, will pursue his principles unto death."*
>
> -Thomas Paine

Thomas Paine battled for equal rights and freedom and devoted much of his life to this very worthy cause. He lived his life with intensity and conviction, though his later years would prove to greatly diminish him. We can be grateful for his contributions to the great cause of liberty and mourn the personal failings that led to his demise.

Discussion

Thomas Paine did not seem to care much about how others viewed his writings. He just wrote what he believed. Do you think this was the right way for him to be? Why do you think it was or wasn't? What were his main convictions? Do you think his upbringing in England had anything to do with his strong beliefs? Paine's later writing that attacked the Bible and Christianity caused many to turn away from his support. Do you think people can honor someone for one thing, and reject his beliefs on something else? Does it make you think less of the man as a whole? Discuss your thoughts with your parent or teacher.

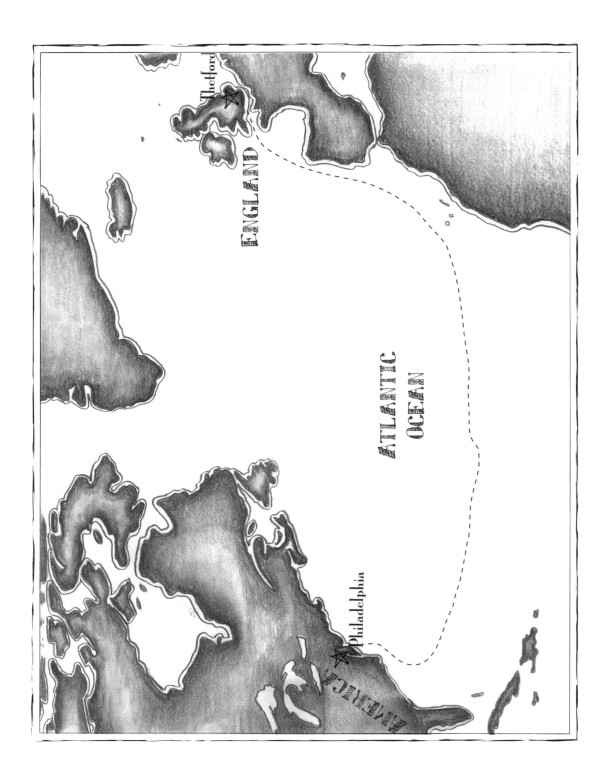

Timeline Review

Put things in perspective. Place Thomas Paine's figure on the timeline in the year 1776, which was when his booklet *Common Sense* was published. Look at the other events before, during, and after this year.

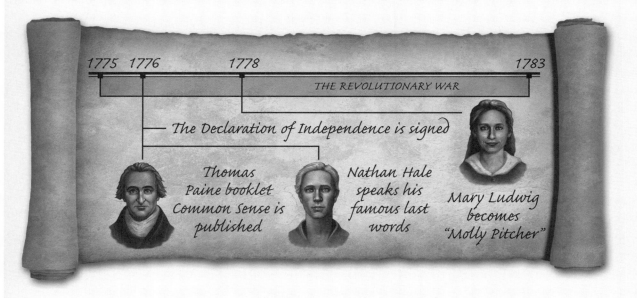

Activity

Talk with your parent or teacher about each quote given in this section from Thomas Paine's writings. Tell your teacher or parent what you think each one of them means. Choose your favorite and practice reading it aloud. Present it to your family, class, or group. Read it expressively, the way you believe Thomas Paine might have spoken it.

Wordscramble

Here is a list of scrambled words that relate to the profile you read about Thomas Paine. Unscramble the letters and write the words correctly.

1. omnaTiPsaeh _____

2. ynynart_____

3. lmhtappe _____

4. CsSonmeemno_____

5. hresisiCT _____

6. Esmnhelign _____

7. htRifanToegMhs _____

8. GnnWetoogrihegsa_____

9. rnespii _____

10. iointnccvo _____

Using Context

Read the sentence and then look at the word in *italics*. Tell what you think that word means. Then look it up in a dictionary to confirm, or make sure of, the meaning. Tell someone about each word that you got correct. Remember, you will get better at understanding word meanings as you practice using context, or the words around a word.

1. There are still countries today that live under such *tyranny*. (paragraph 2)

   I think *tyranny* means: _____

   Dictionary definition: _____

   My meaning was: (Circle one)   correct   had correct parts   not close

2. He could *inspire* people with just his words. (paragraph 5)

   I think *inspire* means: _____

   Dictionary definition: _____

   My meaning was: (Circle one)   correct   had correct parts   not close

3. At the very least, he lived his life with *conviction*, and that is more than many can say. (paragraph 10)

   I think *conviction* means: _____

   Dictionary definition: _____

   My meaning was: (Circle one)   correct   had correct parts   not close

Thomas Paine Word Search

```
Q Y T H P N M I T D W C A P Z F Y S B
M C G P A W E O L C F O P I A D N P E
V T N N M G M C Y Q L M B F R I C B N
K V M G P Q Z I S H W M I S S U O M G
Q L T Y H H X D J M N O K S D G N D L
L X L N L Z L U N T U N I I X C V F I
X U O N E W I U G D Q S Y X N J I Q S
U Z V Y T Y R A N N Y E H W K W C L H
G E O R G E W A S H I N G T O N T T M
C J N C J J B Q C F F S P C D L I B E
V J P M D S U L E D F E V W G W O T N
P T H E C R I S I S K U K X S H N Q J
P K P T H E R I G H T S O F M A N O Q
W N I N S P I R E A C J L A N B R C U
T H O M A S P A I N E K N E S Y C K R
```

Word Bank

Common Sense

conviction

Englishmen

George Washington

inspire

pamphlet

The Crisis

The Rights of Man

Thomas Paine

tyranny

Thomas Paine Crossword

Across

3. pamphlet that resulted in Paine's rejection by his homeland
6. important pamphlet written before the Revolutionary War
7. a small booklet that gives an author's position on an issue
8. to write or speak words that encourage or strengthen others
9. men born in England

Down

1. rule over others with cruel or unjust power
2. leader who read *The Crisis* to his troops
3. author of works promoting individual freedom and liberty
4. inspirational pamphlet written during the Revolutionary War
5. a firmly held belief

Nathan Hale

In the world today, when you turn twenty-one years old, most people your age are almost ready to graduate from college. Some have yet to go to college, and others are looking for their first "real" jobs. In any case, twenty-one year olds have only just begun to live. They feel young and know they have the rest of their lives to decide what they are going to do.

The year 1776 was a completely different circumstance. If you were twenty-one years old and male, you had probably enlisted in the Continental Army. For one young man, twenty-one years were all he had to live, and even though his life was short by today's standards, he gave a story to America that will forever be told as part of its history.

His story is one of sacrifice, dignity, and courage. It started when he volunteered to become a soldier at the very beginning of the War of Independence. American volunteers in this war realized that their rivals not only outnumbered them, but were well-trained in combat compared to the many farmers, teachers, and blacksmiths who opposed them. Nathan Hale was among the teachers who joined. He was young and bright, and promotion through the ranks to Captain in the Rangers came quickly. This unit was famous for bravery on dangerous missions.

In the Battle of Long Island, New York, with its deep harbor, was Britain's next target to conquer. There they would have the opportunity to protect the entire British fleet. If they succeeded in capturing New York, they could make their way up north to connect with their comrades who were close by in Canada. The colonists knew that this was an important battle. Therefore, Nathan Hale willingly volunteered for his last mission. It was an intelligence-gathering mission in which he disguised himself as a Dutch schoolmaster. He made valuable notes and sketches of British positions. If he had not been caught, the information gathered would have been priceless to the colonial army. On September 21, the very night that he planned to go back, the enemy captured him. Betrayed by the information that he had gathered, he knew what his fate would be.

Nathan's commendable school statistics didn't make him famous; nor did his decorated service in the Continental Army. It was that on the fateful day, September 22, 1776, America found a hero. It happened when a British officer named William Cunningham asked Nathan to make his final "speech and confession" just before he was hanged.

His reply: "I only regret that I have but one life to lose for my country." These immortal words have lived on to inspire generation after generation of American soldiers. A statue at the Central Intelligence Agency (CIA) headquarters in Virginia commemorates Nathan as America's first spy.

The definition of the word patriot is "a person who vigorously supports his country and is prepared to defend it against enemies or detractors." Nathan Hale was a patriot to the fullest extent of the word. He freely gave the ultimate sacrifice for his country at a time when many would have begged for his or her life. Nathan Hale died with dignity and courage and left a lasting impression on America.

Discussion

Even though Nathan Hale was young, he had many qualities that made him an excellent soldier. Talk with your teacher or parent about what those qualities were. There is still a unit in the army called the Rangers. Learn more about this unit and what it takes to be a part of it. Do you think Nathan Hale would still fit in this unit today?

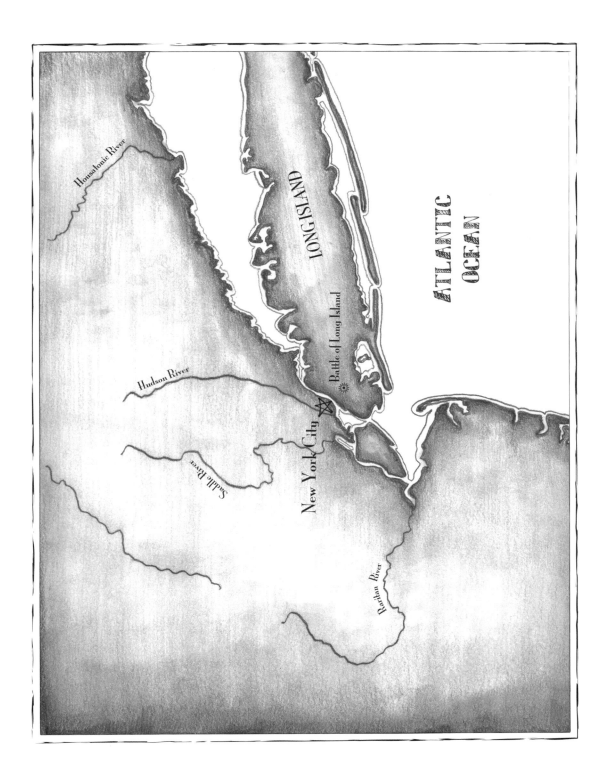

Timeline Review

Put things in perspective. Place Nathan Hale's figure on the timeline in the year 1776, which was when he spoke his famous last words. Look at the other events before, during and after this year

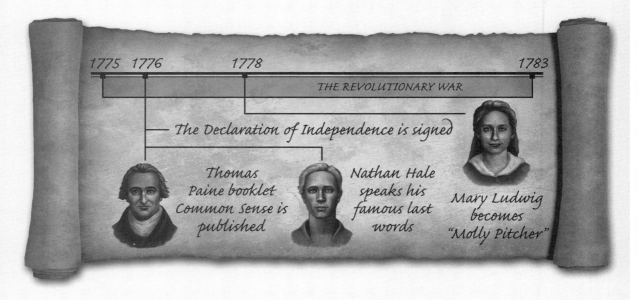

1775 1776   1778   1783

THE REVOLUTIONARY WAR

— The Declaration of Independence is signed

Thomas Paine booklet Common Sense is published

Nathan Hale speaks his famous last words

Mary Ludwig becomes "Molly Pitcher"

Activity

With your parent's permission, talk with someone who is a soldier, or who has recently been a soldier. Tell him or her about the story of Nathan Hale. Does the soldier know of anyone like Nathan Hale in the service now? Find out if the soldier thinks that Nathan's age was then or is now a problem for soldiers. Make sure and thank the soldier for his or her service to the country.

Wordscramble

Here is a list of scrambled words that relate to the profile you read about Nathan Hale. Unscramble the letters and write the words correctly.

1. lNaeantHah _____

2. raeecth _____

3. AyelotriCmannnt _____

4. glonnaLsId _____

5. egnaRrs _____

6. yrarbev _____

7. ICA _____

8. erho _____

9. ueorvtenl _____

10. ioptart _____

Using Context

Read the sentence and then look at the word in *italics*. Tell what you think that word means. Then look it up in a dictionary to confirm, or make sure of, the meaning. Tell someone about each word that you got correct. Remember, you will get better at understanding word meanings as you practice using context, or the words around a word.

1. Therefore, Nathan Hale willingly *volunteered* for his last mission. (paragraph 4)

   I think *volunteered* means: _____

   Dictionary definition: _____

   My meaning was: (Circle one)   correct   had correct parts   not close

2. It was that on the fateful day, September 22, 1776, America found a *hero*. (paragraph 5)

   I think *hero* means: _____

   Dictionary definition: _____

   My meaning was: (Circle one)   correct   had correct parts   not close

3. Nathan Hale was a *patriot* to the fullest extent of the word. (paragraph 6)

   I think *patriot* means: _____

   Dictionary definition: _____

   My meaning was: (Circle one)   correct   had correct parts   not close

Nathan Hale Word Search

```
E Z A L V X V W H T X L L J Q N T Y X
T S J P F N Q R A T E Q H L I B R J B
I N H J V X A C M E J H P O W R G P Q
Q Y U K U Z J Y N A T H A N H A L E L
L V P R F U J T X C I A T G X V R T I
Z Q V S C B A E I H Z E R I X E N A L
T H U S U G T V J E K A I S U R U X Z
A E R L F W W I N R T G O L F Y I C I
N R A N G E R S C L A E T A D G C K Y
V O L U N T E E R I D H T N W L M R L
F G F C W V F S W Z I W D D G T D E Q
N V D C O N T I N E N T A L A R M Y Z
D H D Z V Y B S X S J Z J Q S C N T V
I P W N B W F C X S F M H A M C H Q Y
X N S V O O H O E S K F Y F Y L A L S
```

Word Bank

bravery
CIA
Continental Army
hero
Long Island

Nathan Hale
patriot
Rangers
teacher
volunteer

Nathan Hale Crossword

Across

3. great courage
5. American army
9. someone who shows remarkable bravery or strength of character
10. willingly agree to do something

Down

1. someone who vigorously supports and defends his country
2. Nathan's profession before becoming a soldier
4. Central Intelligence Agency
6. first American spy
7. site of important battle in New York
8. army unit famous for bravery

Mary Ludwig

Mary Ludwig wasn't born famous, nor did she become famous as a writer or as the wife of a president or other political leader. She grew up on a small farm near Trenton, New Jersey. Her name was Mary Ludwig, but everyone just called her Molly. She had an average childhood, doing chores around the farm and helping her parents in any way that she could. So what was it then that Molly did to have her story retold almost 200 years after her death?

Molly was raised to put others before herself. She was taught to be thoughtful, and self-sacrificing. It's no wonder that what she is most remembered for is putting her own life at risk to save the lives of others.

This young woman believed that when a need arose, she would be ready. She knew that there were professions and tasks that a man might be better suited for, but she would never set something aside that she knew she could help with, just because it was not a "woman's job." Molly did what needed to be done in any circumstance. During that time period, women like her, who were determined to serve, made a great difference.

When Molly was a young woman, she worked as a maid in Carlisle, Pennsylvania. While there she married a man named William Hays, who was a barber. William saved Molly from the life of a servant, and the two became inseparable. Several years after they were married, the War for Independence broke out. William enlisted in the artillery, and Molly decided that she would travel to the battles with him. Women who did this during the Revolutionary War were called "Camp Followers." It wasn't an easy life, but for Molly, it was the only choice she was willing to make. She was a patriot so she wanted to help the war effort. Even more than that, she wanted to be there for her husband. Molly would cook meals for the men, mend their clothes, and nurse them when they were sick.

It was June 28, 1778, on a very hot summer day, that Mary Ludwig Hays became forever known as "Molly Pitcher." General Washington had brought his Continental Army to Monmouth, New Jersey, to face the British. As the battle of Monmouth progressed, Molly noticed that some of the men were fainting. They were getting overheated and without some water they might not make it! This was an extraordinarily hot day, combined with heavy uniforms and exhausting combat. Molly knew what needed to be done. She used water from a nearby spring to fill her pitcher, and started bringing it to the men. Amidst bullets and cannon balls, Molly risked her life to bring these fighting men water.

During one of her trips from the spring, Molly noticed William was not at his post. Much to her dismay she found him on the ground next to his cannon. He had either collapsed from heat exhaustion or been wounded. After Molly tended to her husband, making sure that he was going to live, she risked her life yet again. Molly Pitcher earned her place in history that day when she took over her husband's cannon. She had watched William man the cannon before, so she began the complicated process of swabbing, ramming, and firing. Molly knew that without the aid of even this one cannon, the battle could be lost. So she continued to do the grueling work throughout the day until the battle was over.

It is said that when General Washington heard of Molly's courage, he personally thanked her for her service—and even made her a sergeant, right then and there. That we do not know for sure. But what we do know is that the Pennsylvania legislature eventually gave Molly an annual pension of forty dollars, "for services rendered during the Revolutionary War."

Molly Pitcher was an average, fairly poor woman, who likely didn't have any kind of formal education. The daughter of a dairy farmer, she later married a barber. But Molly's actions have forever placed her with a unique group in history. She was brave, gallant, selfless, and above all else a true heroine. Because of her love for her husband and country, Molly did what most anyone else would have cowered at just the thought of. Her story will, without a doubt, inspire untold generations to risk a little more, to help a little longer, and to be just a little extra brave.

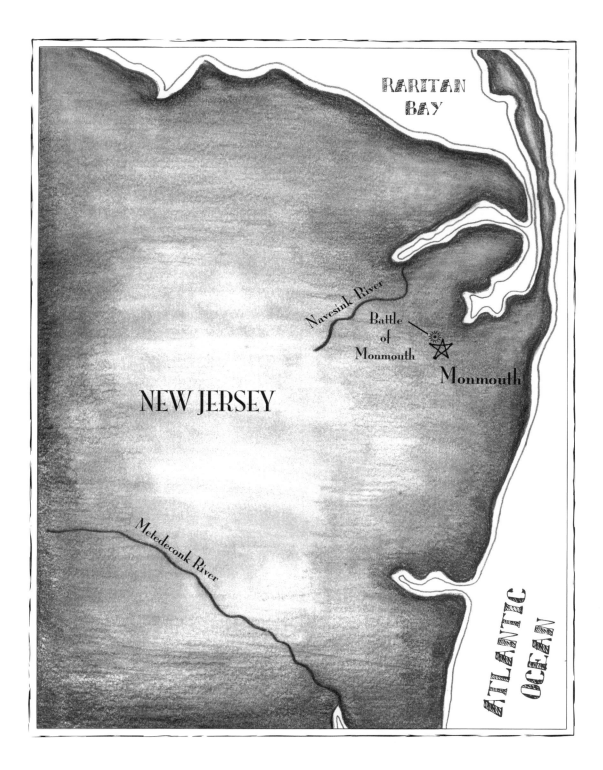

RARITAN BAY

Navesink River

Battle
of
Monmouth

Monmouth

NEW JERSEY

Metedeconk River

ATLANTIC OCEAN

Discussion

Molly's devotion to her husband and her country led her to serve in a way that was not widely known. Many women and children followed their husbands and fathers into battle, caring for them and others. Their service was rewarded with rations from the troop, and protection. Some didn't want to be left behind when the British attacked, without the protection of their men. Life was hard, and they had to keep up with the troop as they traveled. Yet for many camp followers, this was the best place to be. Talk with your parent or teacher about the life they lived. Do you agree with their decision to become camp followers? Do you think you would become a camp follower if the same thing happened to you? Why or why not?

Timeline Review

Put things in perspective. Place Mary Ludwig's figure on the timeline in the year 1778, when she became "Molly Pitcher" at the battle of Monmouth. Look at the other events before, during, and after this year.

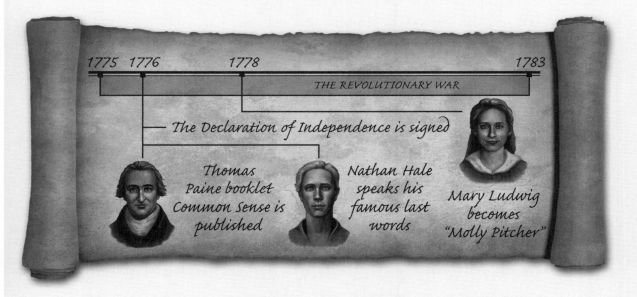

1775 1776   1778   1783

THE REVOLUTIONARY WAR

The Declaration of Independence is signed

Thomas Paine booklet Common Sense is published

Nathan Hale speaks his famous last words

Mary Ludwig becomes "Molly Pitcher"

Activity

Learn about what it took to fire a cannon in Revolutionary War times. Was this an easy task? Tell what the steps were in firing this weapon. What materials and strength did it take to man, or fire a cannon? Why do you think cannon fire was so important during a battle?

Draw a cannon, or the steps it took to fire one. Is this a job you would have liked to have?

Before and After

Read the event on the left side and the event on the right side. Then decide if the first event (on the left) happened **before** or **after** the second event (on the right). Choose the word in the middle column that is correct. You may circle the correct answer or draw a line from the words *before* or *after* to the matching event.

1	Molly became a camp follower.	Before	After	Molly lived on a small farm.
2	She helped her parents any way she could.	Before	After	Molly married William Hays.
3	William enlisted in the artillery during the Revolutionary War.	Before	After	The Battle of Monmouth was fought on a very hot day.
4	Molly brought the soldiers water during battle.	Before	After	She took responsibility for firing the cannon when her husband was injured.
5	She was awarded a pension from the state of Pennsylvania.	Before	After	Molly noticed that men were fainting on the battlefield.

Mary Ludwig Word Search

```
E Z A L V X V W H T X L L J Q N T M X
T S J P F N Q R A H E Q H I I K R A B
I C A N N O N C M E J H G W W H G R Q
Q A U K U Z J Y H R Z G B G T R V Y L
L M O N M O U T H O S S H B X S R L I
Z P V S C B A E I I Z E E E X R N U L
T F U S U G T V J N K A G C U N U D Z
A O R L F W W I N E T G H L F Y I W I
N L C B R Y P B C L A E U V D G C I Y
B L H R N Z H I X I D H T D W L M G L
M O L L Y P I T C H E R D S G T D H Q
N W I L L I A M H A Y S M K L R S A Z
S E L F L E S S X S J Z J Q S C N Y V
B R A V E W F C X S F M H A M C H S Y
X N G E O R G E W A S H I N G T O N S
```

Word Bank

brave
camp follower
cannon
George Washington
heroine

Mary Ludwig Hays
Molly Pitcher
Monmouth
selfless
William Hays

Mary Ludwig Crossword

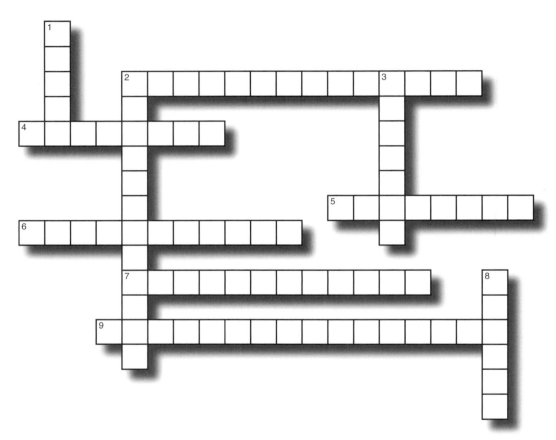

Across

2. Molly Pitcher's real name
4. putting other people's needs or interests before your own
5. site and name of the battle where Molly Pitcher got her name
6. Molly Pitcher's husband
7. someone who followed troops into war
9. Commander of the Continental Army

Down

1. having or showing courage
2. woman who manned a cannon in the Revolutionary War
3. a woman who shows remarkable bravery or strength of character
8. a large weapon that fired heavy iron balls

Samuel Adams

Let me paint a picture for you. Imagine yourself at the Green Dragon Tavern in Boston, sitting next to Samuel Adams sometime during the years that led up to the Revolutionary War. Undoubtedly, he would have struck up a conversation about politics. Sam loved politics more than anything else. He would have told you how unreasonable it was for England and its King to attempt to tell the American people what to do. "Who are they to try to control us," he would say. "Independence is what we need, even if we have to fight for it!"

Samuel Adams devoted his life to fighting for it. Some have called him the "Father of the American Revolution." He began opposing British rule at a time when it wasn't the popular choice to make. He was one of the first men who started turning people's minds toward revolution.

Adams was born and grew up in Boston, Massachusetts, so the city and its people were always close to his heart. His family was politically active, and at 14 he went to Harvard College, which was near Boston. He worked hard to pay his own way through college. He didn't have the best clothes or the nicest things, but that never mattered to him. He was among a few outstanding men who put their personal concerns aside and changed our country forever.

His political career began when he and some friends started a weekly newspaper called *The Public Adviser*. It was through this newspaper that Samuel's passionate and bold opinions were heard. He once said, "It does not require a majority to prevail, but rather an irate, tireless minority keen to set brush fires in people's minds." He was right, and that is what he set out to do. One brush fire after another, he told anyone who would listen about his beliefs. Even the British called him an incendiary, which means someone who is likely to light a fire of opinion among the people, and cause unrest. In a fight for freedom, he was just the kind of person America needed.

Adams encouraged people to protest, rebel, and stand up against injustice! Well known for being an agitator, he did his best to stir people up. He was so influential that an English Governor offered him all the comforts he could ever want, if he would only stop what he was doing. As we know, Sam's strong moral convictions and his passion would never allow him to take such an offer.

One of the more important contributions Samuel Adams made to our freedom was that he organized the first Committee of Correspondence. He knew it was only through unity that the American people could overcome a more capable, wealthy, and experienced opponent. So he organized a way for everyone to stay connected to the latest happenings on the political scene. After the Boston Massacre, Adams wanted to make sure that America did not forget what had happened. He wrote over forty articles in just a two-year period expressing his opinions and keeping people informed of the current events.

The story of the Revolutionary War has always been one of outnumbered and oftentimes less capable, but impassioned, patriots. Without passion, without hope and fierce motivation, the war for independence could have ended very differently. Adams knew this. When even the leaders, those in the most critical positions, began to lose faith, Samuel Adams didn't falter. He refused to give up hope. These were his words:

> *"The chance is desperate. Indeed, indeed, it is desperate, if this be our language. If we wear long faces, others will do so too; if we despair, let us not expect that others will hope; or that they will persevere in a contest, from which their leaders shrink. But let not such feelings, let not such language, be ours."*

Samuel Adams was a statesman, a political philosopher, one of America's Founding Fathers, a signer of the Declaration of Independence, leader of the Boston Tea Party and a member of the Continental Congress. He helped draft the Articles of Confederation, was president of the Massachusetts senate, Lieutenant Governor, and finally, Governor of Massachusetts from 1794 to 1797.

I will let one who knew him much better than I, John Adams (cousin to Samuel Adams and the second president of the United States,) have the final words on this outstanding American:

> *"Without the character of Samuel Adams, the true history of the American Revolution can never be written. For fifty years his pen, his tongue, his activity were constantly exerted for his country without fee or reward."*

-John Adams

Discussion

Sam Adams loved politics, or the theories and practices that relate to government. Finish this statement: The best thing I think the government has done recently is

_____.

Ask your parents and other family members and friends if they agree with your statement. Ask them how they would finish that statement. Now you are talking politics! Notice if everyone agrees with you or not. How do you feel if they disagree with you? Did it change your opinion?

Try this again later with a different question, such as: "The worst thing I think the government has done recently is _____,"
and see what happens. You may want to write about what you learn.

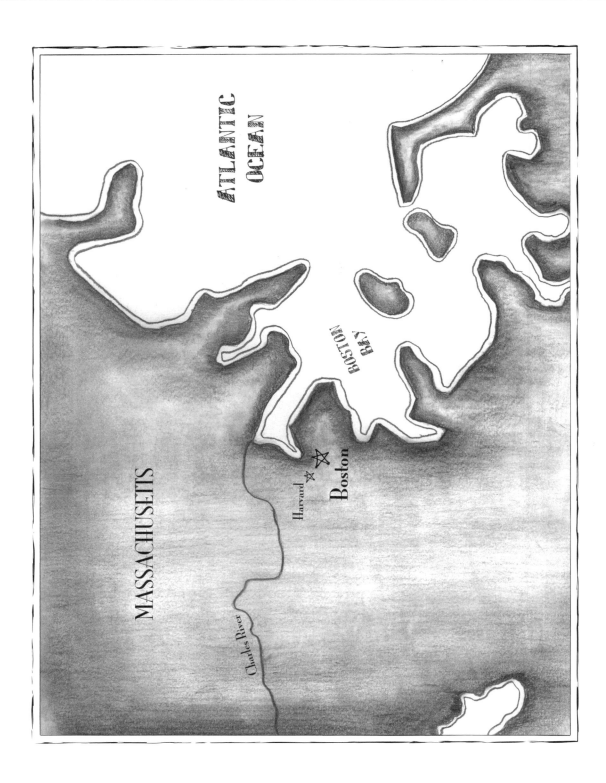

Timeline Review

Put things in perspective. Place Samuel Adams' figure on the timeline in the year 1794, which was when he became Governor of Massachusetts. Look at the other events before, during, and after this year.

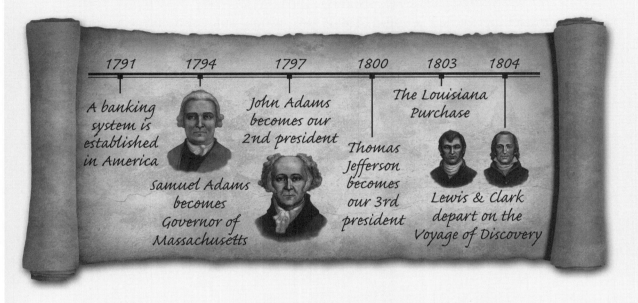

1791 — A banking system is established in America

1794 — Samuel Adams becomes Governor of Massachusetts

1797 — John Adams becomes our 2nd president

1800 — Thomas Jefferson becomes our 3rd president

1803 — The Louisiana Purchase

1804 — Lewis & Clark depart on the Voyage of Discovery

Activity

The Boston Tea Party (when colonists dressed as Indians and dumped tea into Boston Harbor) was an action taken by people who felt their ruler, King George of England, was not listening to their opinions about government rules and taxation. In 2009, a movement was started called the Tea Party Movement. People who felt that leaders were not listening to their opinions about government rules and taxation began it. Learn more about the Tea Party Movement and decide whether you agree with their beliefs.

Wordscramble

Here is a list of scrambled words that relate to the profile you read about Samuel Adams. Unscramble the letters and write the words correctly.

1. aAmSsdlumae _____
2. tgtoraia _____
3. nAmhdsaoJ _____
4. tsnBoo _____
5. intAleRiamnvoucroe _____

6. aradrHv _____
7. hacuesMssatts _____
8. ptclsioi _____
9. onTsrtaayeoPtB _____
10. nepdncneedie _____

Before and After

Read the event on the left side and the event on the right side. Then decide if the first event (on the left) happened **before** or **after** the second event (on the right). Choose the word in the middle column that is correct. You may circle the correct answer or draw a line from the words *before* or *after* to the matching event.

1	Samuel Adams spoke out against the decisions of the King of England.	Before	After	The Revolutionary War began.
2	Samuel organized the first Committee of Correspondence to spread news of events in Boston.	Before	After	Samuel attended Harvard College.
3	The Revolutionary War began.	Before	After	The Boston Tea Party took place.
4	Samuel signed the Declaration of Independence.	Before	After	Samuel became the Governor of Massachusetts.
5	Samuel's cousin John was elected President.	Before	After	Samuel encouraged the patriots to continue fighting.

Samuel Adams Word Search

```
E Z A L V X V B O S T O N J Q N T Y X
T S J P F N Q R A A I Q H I I K R J B
I N H O V X A C M M N H G W W H G P Q
Q H U L U Z J J H U D G B G T R V J L
L A G I T A T O R E E S H B X S R T I
Z R V T C B A H I L P E E X R N A L
T V U I U G T N J A E A G C U N U X Z
A A R C F W W A N D N G H L F Y I C I
N R C S R Y P D C A D E U V D G C K Y
B D H R N Z H A X M E H T D W L M R L
F G F C W V F M W S N W D S G T D E Q
N V D V I M A S S A C H U S E T T S Z
D H D B O S T O N T E A P A R T Y T V
A M E R I C A N R E V O L U T I O N Y
X N S V O O H O E S K F Y F Y L A L S
```

Word Bank

agitator

American Revolution

Boston

Boston Tea Party

Harvard

independence

John Adams

Massachusetts

politics

Samuel Adams

Samuel Adams Crossword

Across

2. protest of government rules and taxation
3. theories and practices that relate to government
4. "Father of the American Revolution"
5. Samuel's home state, where he was later Governor
9. war that led to American independence
10. cousin to Samuel Adams and second President

Down

1. freedom from control by another person or government
6. someone who stirs up feelings for or against something
7. the university Samuel attended near Boston
8. Samuel's hometown in Massachusetts

John Adams

John Adams was one of the most virtuous and underrated of our Founding Fathers. He was the kind of man that Americans can look back on and hold their heads a little higher. A lawyer, Adams saw right and wrong very clearly. He never failed to stand on the side of integrity, even when it threatened to cost him everything. As our second President, he saved the United States from an impending war with the French by using diplomacy. Before becoming President, he was Vice-President to the great George Washington for two terms.

John Adams grew up in a town near Boston called Braintree. He was the oldest son and therefore it was determined that he be well-educated. John's brothers helped around the farm while he attended school each day. With his father's encouragement, John studied diligently and was accepted into Harvard College at the age of fifteen. He made his family proud by working very hard at Harvard and graduating third in his class.

After graduation, Adams was offered a job teaching in a town nearby. He taught for only a year. It was long enough, however, for him to decide that teaching was not what he wanted to do with the rest of his life. Finally, after much consideration, John decided he wanted to become a lawyer. He wanted to make a difference in people's lives and in the community. Little did he know that he would make a great difference!

When he was in his late twenties, Adams married a young woman by the name of Abigail Smith. Abigail proved to be the ideal partner of his life in many ways. She was strong, gentle, intelligent, and full of life and conviction. She was undoubtedly a crucial addition to John's wisdom and success. She is now remembered almost as fondly, if not more so, than her husband. Together they had five children. One of them, John Quincy Adams, would later become the sixth President of the United States.

Adams was always interested in politics. He watched right along with the town of Boston as the British Parliament kept handing down more taxes and more laws that encroached upon their freedoms. From the very beginning, he thought that if the colonies ever united against this foreign ruler, they would undoubtedly be able to defeat it. Every time Adams was selected to be a delegate, or representative of the people, he was always surprised. He would marvel at the little experience and knowledge he considered himself to have compared to others. But the people around him could see the truth. They could see the wisdom and intelligence behind his kind eyes.

The so-called "Boston Massacre" that became so famous was actually an accident in which a crowd of people was antagonizing several British soldiers. Eventually the crowd was fired upon when one of the soldiers (after being hit with a club) thought that their captain had yelled "fire"—but it was actually a random person who shouted that fatal word. It might have been someone in the crowd, or one of the other soldiers who yelled out. No one knows. Five people died in this unfortunate event, though it was hardly a massacre. Some patriots took the opportunity to fan the flame of revolution. Only one person had the courage to look at both sides of the tragedy. John Adams stood up against his fellow patriots, his friends, and even his relatives to follow his conscience.

After the massacre, a local merchant visited Adams and pleaded for him to defend the soldiers. After hearing their side of the story, Adams knew what the right thing to do was. He wouldn't, no he couldn't, stand by and watch innocent men be condemned. So John Adams, against popular opinion, defended the British soldiers and their Captain in the Boston court of law.

It was due to his excellent representation and dedicated work that the Captain and six of his soldiers were completely acquitted of all charges. The jury only convicted two soldiers of manslaughter, which was accurate and a lesser sentence than murder. Many years later, after having been paid almost nothing for his work, Adams said this of the case:

"It was one of the most gallant, generous, manly, and disinterested (meaning not in his self-interest) actions of my whole life, and one of the best pieces of service I ever rendered my country."

John Adams was the first person to propose the three separate branches of government that are still in use today. They are the legislative, executive, and judicial branches. He wrote his ideas out in a pamphlet called *Thoughts on Government.* John Adams had an amazing ability to organize. He could organize people, the many ideas that came from the Continental Congress, and ways to implement plans. Without his decisive encouragement, some plans might have taken much longer to be put into action. He gave up much of his time and energy to helping establish the United States government. He knew that this was the most crucial time in our country's development and wanted to help in whatever way he could. Even his wife Abigail could see the importance and supported her husband through all of his time spent away from home. They stayed as connected as two people could be through the written word. Letters back and forth became their lifeline. Visits were treasured, and later on when Adams retired back to his hometown in Braintree, the simple life was never considered so sweet.

Adams was one of only five men who were chosen to draft the Declaration of Independence. He was selected as a delegate to the First and Second Continental Congresses. As a very active member of Congress, John was chairman of twenty-five committees as well as serving on countless others. Along with his accomplishments and services to our country, Adams' letters and illuminating diary are among America's greatest historical treasures from that time. He eloquently gave us a window into his feelings, his troubles, and his joys. John Adams gave his country all of the knowledge and wisdom he had to offer. He worked tirelessly to give America a foundation on which to build. Dedicating his life and his time to our future, this country will forever be in his debt.

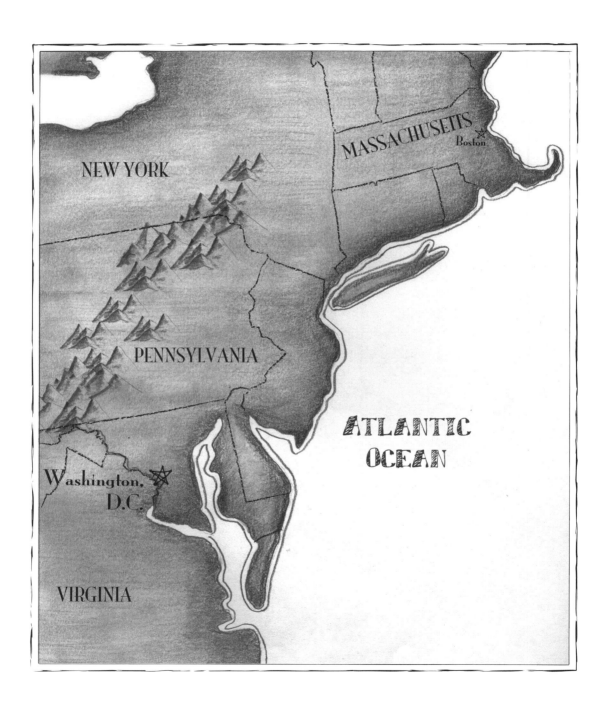

Timeline Review

Put things in perspective. Place John Adams' figure on the timeline in the year 1796, which was when he became our 2nd president. Look at the other events before, during, and after this year.

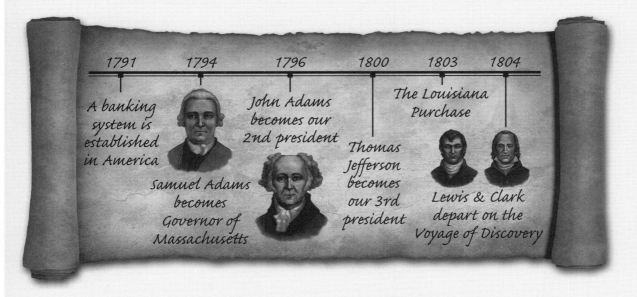

Activity

Read about several laws in your state. Tell your teacher or parent what benefit you think those laws give to the citizens in your state. Also tell what you think would happen if people in your state did not follow the law, or if only some people followed the law? What would happen? (For example, there are traffic laws that every citizen has to follow. What would happen if no one stopped at a red light? What would happen if only a few people stopped at a red light?) Think of a law that you would like to create. How would it benefit people? Would everyone need to follow the law? What would happen to those who didn't follow the law?

Discussion

John Adams was in a difficult situation. After the Boston Massacre, people wanted to punish the British soldiers involved before a trial could determine if they were guilty. John Adams believed the British soldiers deserved a fair trial, even though he did not support their reasons for being there. He believed in the rule of law, which means that laws should apply to everyone equally. Why do you think it was especially important for John Adams to stay true to his beliefs about the importance of the rule of law in the case of the British soldiers? Should we apply laws based on how we feel about those who break the law? What would that do to our country, if people were never sure when laws would be applied fairly or not?

Wordscramble

Here is a list of scrambled words that relate to the profile you read about John Adams. Unscramble the letters and write the words correctly.

1. nadAosmJh _____

2. tiretgyni _____

3. rHrvaad _____

4. cnicsceneo _____

5. imslaaAgiAdb _____

6. dnyhsuJmiaQnAco _____

7. raelwy _____

8. rculcia _____

9. eMoatscBsraosn _____

10. neterBria _____

Using Context

Read the sentence and then look at the word in *italics*. Tell what you think that word means. Then look it up in a dictionary to confirm, or make sure of, the meaning. Tell someone about each word that you got correct. Remember, you will get better at understanding word meanings as you practice using context, or the words around a word.

1. He never failed to stand on the side of *integrity*, even when it threatened to cost him everything. (paragraph 1)

   I think *integrity* means: _____

   Dictionary definition: _____

   My meaning was: (Circle one)   correct   had correct parts   not close

2. John Adams stood up against his fellow patriots, his friends and even his relatives to follow his *conscience*. (paragraph 6)

   I think *conscience* means: _____

   Dictionary definition: _____

   My meaning was: (Circle one)   correct   had correct parts   not close

3. He knew that this was the most crucial time in our country's development and wanted to help in whatever way he could. (paragraph 10)

   I think *crucial* means: _____

   Dictionary definition: _____

   My meaning was: (Circle one)   correct   had correct parts   not close

John Adams Word Search

```
E J O H N Q U I N C Y A D A M S T Y X
T S B R A I N T R E E Q H I I K R J B
I N H J B X A C M I J H G W W H G P Q
Q Y U K I Z J Y H N Z G B G T R V J L
L C P R G U J T X T S S H B X S R T I
J O H N A D A M S E Z E E E X R N A L
T N U S I G T V J G K L G C U N U X Z
A S R L L W W H A R V A R D F Y I C I
N C C B A Y P B C I A W U V D G C K Y
B I H R D Z H I X T D Y T D W L M R L
F E F C A V F S W Y I E D S G T D E Q
N N D V M C B Z S K C R U C I A L H Z
D C B O S T O N M A S S A C R E N T V
I E W N B W F C X S F M H A M C H Q Y
X N S V O O H O E S K F Y F Y L A L S
```

Word Bank

Abigail Adams
Boston Massacre
Braintree
conscience
crucial

Harvard
integrity
John Adams
John Quincy Adams
lawyer

John Adams Crossword

Across

2. the second President of the United States
3. son of John Adams, sixth President of the United States
5. having great impact to how something turns out
8. wife of John Adams, mother of John Quincy Adams

Down

1. a skirmish between colonists and the British in which five were killed
4. John Adams' hometown in Massachusetts
6. a person's guiding sense of right and wrong
7. the college attended by John Adams
9. devotion to high standards and principles
10. someone who is qualified to advise and represent others in court

Dolley Madison

What do you think of when you imagine a First Lady of the United States? Do you picture someone who is gracious, intelligent, and elegant, has a passion for her country and a desire to help people in need? Who was the first First Lady to use her position in such a way that everyone after her had a standard to measure up to? Her name was Dolley Madison. She was the wife of our fourth president James Madison, whom many refer to as the "Father of the Constitution."

Dolley's influence first began when President Thomas Jefferson asked her to be the hostess for White House events. Sadly, Jefferson was a widower, and his adult daughters lived with their own families in central Virginia. Dolley willingly agreed to help. Her husband James, a friend of Jefferson's, was Secretary of State at the time. While Dolley was the "unofficial" First Lady, she took on a considerable public role in support of the fundraising effort for Lewis and Clark's famous Western expedition.

After Jefferson, James Madison became the next President of the United States. Dolley and James originally met through a mutual friend when she was 25, and even though James was 17 years older than she, they were wed within weeks of meeting. They were happily married for 42 years, and only separated by James' death in 1836. She is said to have been a very pleasant and necessary contrast to James' reserved personality. It was Dolley who smoothed over political tensions with her gracious and calming persona. She hosted many dinner parties while in Washington and was famous for her Wednesday evening receptions that various politicians, diplomats, and even regular citizens attended. Not only did she entertain, but she also used social opportunities to gain knowledge of possible future difficulties for the Madison administration, and to try to persuade those who opposed her husband's agenda. Some people think that without her public influence James might never have been re-elected for his second term. Dolley was also the first President's wife to aid a charitable organization. She helped to found a home for young orphaned girls in Washington, D.C.

One of her greatest contributions to this country happened during the War of 1812. While British troops were closing in on Washington, Dolley was directed to evacuate to a safer location. Before she would leave though, she made sure they saved as many of her husband's important documents and books as they could, along with a most cherished American artifact—Gilbert Stuart's portrait of George Washington. Unaffected by her title, the First Lady helped right along with the servants to load and secure the important items. Showing her patriotism and bravery, who knows what would have been lost if Dolley hadn't refused to leave.

Before Dolley Madison, Presidents' wives were much quieter in their support. Since Dolley, being First Lady has become a very important and influential role. So many First Ladies have accomplished great things. You could say that it goes back to one person, the first of the First Ladies to inspire a new institution—one that demonstrates patriotism, encourages selflessness, and motivates people to represent their country with pride.

Discussion

When guests felt comfortable and welcomed by Dolley Madison, they tended to be more cooperative in political matters. Thus, she used her talent for hospitality to benefit the country. Everyone has gifts and talents that make them unique and special. When we try to merely copy the skills of others, we may set aside a needed or appreciated talent. Talk with your teacher or parent about the importance of each person doing what he or she does best. What do you think your talents and gifts are? How can you use them, even as a young person, to help others or bring out the best in them?

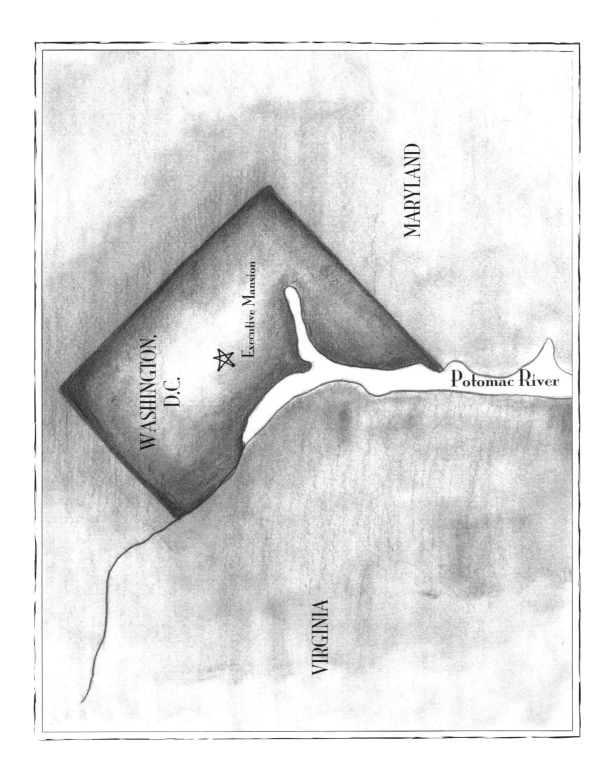

Timeline Review

Put things in perspective. Place Dolley Madison's figure on the timeline in the year 1808, which was when she became the First Lady. Look at the other events before, during, and after this year.

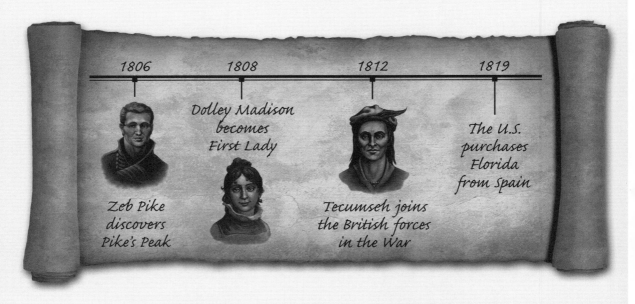

1806 — Zeb Pike discovers Pike's Peak

1808 — Dolley Madison becomes First Lady

1812 — Tecumseh joins the British forces in the War

1819 — The U.S. purchases Florida from Spain

Activity

When Dolley Madison first became the official hostess for the White House, she was a young woman. She was able to focus on the needs of the White House rather than the needs of small children, as was the case with previous First Ladies. Her personality and talents led her to gain a reputation for hospitality. While it may seem frivolous or unimportant to some, she certainly demonstrated that the atmosphere you create in a home makes a big difference. Talk with your teacher or parent about what hospitality is, and how you can be more hospitable to those who visit your home. Together with your family, make a plan to be a host or hostess to guests.

Wordscramble

Here is a list of scrambled words that relate to the profile you read about Dolley Madison. Unscramble the letters and write the words correctly.

1. nleaodisDolMy _____

2. sadiseoMJmna _____

3. eTesonafohmsfrJ _____

4. LiraFtsdy _____

5. W118af2or _____

6. plotsici _____

7. DnasnCtiWhog _____

8. hestsso _____

9. GSrtieutbtalr _____

10. ittosunnCiot _____

Before and After

Read the event on the left side and the event on the right side. Then decide if the first event (on the left) happened **before** or **after** the second event (on the right). Choose the word in the middle column that is correct. You may circle the correct answer or draw a line from the words *before* or *after* to the matching event.

1	Thomas Jefferson's wife died.	Before	After	Dolley Madison served as hostess for President Jefferson.
2	James Madison became the 4th President.	Before	After	James Madison served as Secretary of State.
3	Dolley Madison earned a reputation for being hospitable.	Before	After	James Madison was elected to a second term as President.
4	The War of 1812 began.	Before	After	Gilbert Stuart painted a famous portrait of George Washington.
5	The British attacked the white House.	Before	After	Important papers, books and artifacts were removed from the White House.

Dolley Madison Word Search

```
N  A  P  W  U  W  A  S  H  I  N  G  T  O  N  D  C  V  P
Q  U  T  Z  D  W  I  P  F  C  O  I  M  Y  G  F  M  I  B
B  C  Z  P  O  L  I  T  I  C  S  L  J  S  Y  C  N  W  Z
C  V  Z  E  L  O  B  V  R  P  V  B  O  M  P  L  L  J  I
K  K  X  U  L  C  G  S  S  P  F  E  Z  Q  U  P  Z  P  H
M  H  Y  R  E  N  C  Y  T  W  A  R  O  F  1  8  1  2  S
O  G  Q  Y  Y  D  S  F  L  S  T  T  N  K  O  D  F  J  B
H  Q  J  A  M  E  S  M  A  D  I  S  O  N  D  C  X  J  M
I  G  G  H  A  Y  H  Z  D  F  V  T  Q  Q  T  U  B  O  X
A  P  T  J  D  J  U  W  Y  T  B  U  M  M  I  O  X  I  S
L  J  Q  V  I  X  K  W  H  P  Y  A  S  V  D  K  T  S  H
G  M  Z  Q  S  B  U  N  N  D  N  R  U  Y  E  K  I  K  M
Y  I  D  H  O  S  T  E  S  S  I  T  M  D  J  B  R  W  J
Y  D  C  O  N  S  T  I  T  U  T  I  O  N  Q  F  R  S  F
D  L  T  H  O  M  A  S  J  E  F  F  E  R  S  O  N  O  A
```

Word Bank

Constitution
Dolley Madison
First Lady
Gilbert Stuart
hostess

James Madison
politics
Thomas Jefferson
War of 1812
Washington, D.C.

Dolley Madison Crossword

Across

2. First Lady during two administrations
4. Third President of the United States
6. a written document outlining the principles of government
8. the capital city of the United States
9. wife or hostess of a president or governor
10. Fourth President of the United States

Down

1. painted a famous portrait of George Washington
3. conflict between the United States and Great Britain
5. a woman who invites, plans for, and entertains guests
7. the beliefs and practices of organizations associated with government

Tecumseh

During an era when there weren't very many heroes to look up to, an unlikely candidate arose out of a dark time. In the United States during the late 1700s and early 1800s, men were fighting over land and power in fierce and cruel ways. It was a war of newcomers to an old territory. Our hero tragically watched his father and older brother get killed by this war. Yet somehow, amidst all the disaster he stepped forward and refused to give in to the brutality of his surroundings. He believed in honor and showing mercy, things that were nearly unheard of at that time.

Remember, before the Pilgrims traveled to this new, free world, the original inhabitants were Indians. Some were hostile toward visitors, and some welcomed new people to trade with. As more and more Europeans came to the New World, trying to escape the oppression of their homes, the Indians realized they had to start fighting for their land if they wanted to keep it. The instinct of man is to rule, to overtake. It has been a pattern throughout history—whenever a country or group of people has grown strong enough, they have usually tried to expand and conquer as much land as possible.

The foreign white man in America was taking over Tecumseh's home. Tecumseh, who was the leader of a Native American nation called the Shawnee, tried to use his influence to rally his people to fight for their land. He traveled endlessly, speaking to various Indian tribes and trying to convince them not to barter land that he believed they didn't have the right to sell. He thought that no one tribe had the right to trade something that belonged to all the Indian nations. Tecumseh wanted the tribes across the country to stand together as one unified front. However, despite his efforts some tribes still decided to trade their land to the newcomers for alcohol and various other luxuries. Tecumseh did all he could to unite his people and inspire them.

When the war of 1812 began, Tecumseh and the warriors he led fought against the United States. They joined forces with a British Major General named Isaac Brock, and Tecumseh helped him win a couple of very key battles. In the siege of Detroit, Tecumseh's shrewd strategy enabled the British and Indian army to prevail. Today, Tecumseh is considered a national hero in Canada because of the aid he gave to the British in order to keep America from invading the north.

Following Brock, Henry Proctor became the new Major General of the British and Indian coalition. Tecumseh soon discovered that this new leader made a habit of retreating. One time, Proctor agreed to meet Tecumseh in Chatham, Ontario, to make a stand against the Americans. When he did not come, it was the last cowardly act that Tecumseh would take. He told Proctor that if the British did not take action soon, Tecumseh and his men would no longer fight alongside them. However, on October 5th, 1813 it was too late. The British and Indian army was found by an American company and defeated at the famous Battle of the Thames. Major General Proctor abandoned the Native Americans when he realized the battle was coming to an unfavorable end.

Although the Americans eventually won the war of 1812, Tecumseh was a valiant enemy who fought and died bravely. He gave his very life for his cause, but not without making a difference first. After the leader of the Indians died, the resistance and effort to unite the tribes seemed to die with him. Perhaps if he had lived, things would have been different. We will never know what could have been, but we can learn from the past.

Have you ever heard the term "your reputation precedes you?" It means that word has spread about who you are to people that you haven't even met. Tecumseh's reputation preceded him throughout America. He was known as a passionate and charismatic leader of the Shawnee people. He was a leader during a time when America was still being shaped into what it is now. Even his enemies respected him.

Looking back through history, we should pay respect to our great adversaries, or those who did not fight on our side, but fought with dignity and valor against us for a reasonable goal. America was and is a great country. Does that mean we always did everything perfectly? No. We must always try to honor what was right, and the people who sometimes stood up against us for it.

Now you know how he died, but these words from Tecumseh tell more than I could ever convey about how he lived:

> *"So live your life that the fear of death can never enter your heart. Trouble no one about their religion; respect others in their view, and demand that they respect yours. Love your life, perfect your life, beautify all things in your life. Seek to make your life long and its purpose in the service of your people.*

> *Prepare a noble death song for the day when you go over the great divide. Always give a word or a sign of salute when meeting or passing a friend, even a stranger, when in a lonely place. Show respect to all people and bow to none. When you arise in the morning, give thanks for the light, for your life, for your strength. Give thanks for your food and for the joy of living. If you see no reason to give thanks, the fault lies only in yourself. Abuse no one and nothing, for abuse turns the wise ones to fools and robs the spirit of its vision.*

> *When it comes your time to die, be not like those whose hearts are filled with fear of death, so that when their time comes they weep and pray for a little more time to live their lives over again in a different way. Sing your death song and die like a hero going home."*

Discussion

The last three paragraphs of this story give us Tecumseh's words to live by. After reading these words, choose at least two statements he makes that you agree with, and talk about ways you could apply them to your life.

George Washington also studied and wrote words to live by. Think of two ways that he and Tecumseh were the same, and at least two ways that he and Tecumseh were different. Do you think that someone can be a great leader of people even if you don't agree with all their beliefs? Do you think someone who is shrewd, charismatic, and valiant would be a good leader? Tell why or why not.

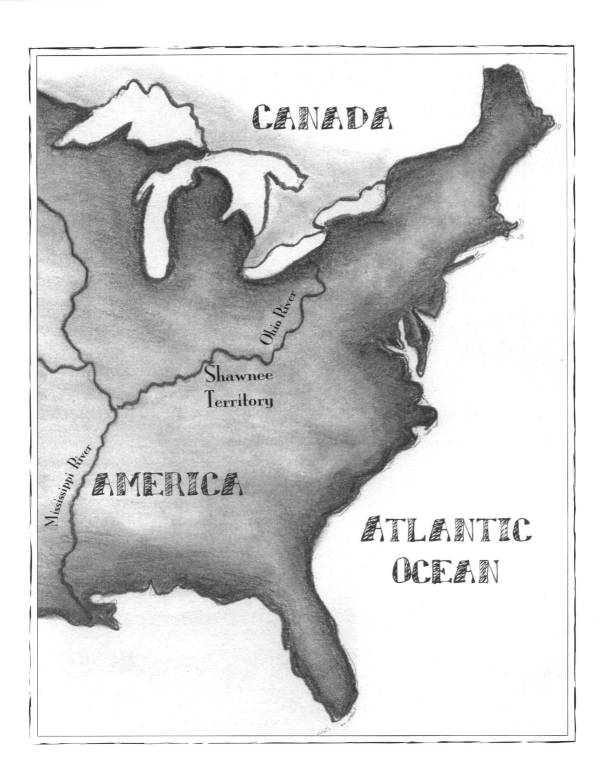

Timeline Review

Put things in perspective. Place Tecumseh's figure on the timeline in the year 1812, which was when he joined the British forces in the War. Look at the other events before, during, and after this year.

1806 — Zeb Pike discovers Pike's Peak

1808 — Dolley Madison becomes First Lady

1812 — Tecumseh joins the British forces in the War

1819 — The U.S. purchases Florida from Spain

Activity

Learn more about the Shawnee nation. Where did they live? Find out what their homes were like and how they provided food for their families. Were the Shawnee warlike or peaceful? Tell your family what you learned. (For information on where they lived, look at the maps entitled "Native American Cultures, 1500s," and "Native American Nations, c. 1750" in the *United States History Atlas*.)

Wordscramble

Here is a list of scrambled words that relate to the profile you read about Tecumseh. Unscramble the letters and write the words correctly.

1. Teucehms _____

2. aSehnwe _____

3. rohno _____

4. erbtra _____

5. esrdwh _____

6. acisihtcmra _____

7. aaitlnv _____

8. anCada _____

9. rtorcoP _____

10. tenuairotp _____

Using Context

Read the sentence and then look at the word in *italics*. Tell what you think that word means. Then look it up in a dictionary to confirm, or make sure of, the meaning. Tell someone about each word that you got correct. Remember, you will get better at understanding word meanings as you practice using context, or the words around a word.

1. In the siege of Detroit, Tecumseh's *shrewd* strategy enabled the British and Indian army to prevail. (paragraph 4)

   I think *shrewd* means: _____

   Dictionary definition: _____

   My meaning was: (Circle one)   correct   had correct parts   not close

2. Although the Americans eventually won the war of 1812, Tecumseh was a *valiant* enemy who fought and died bravely. (paragraph 6)

   I think *valiant* means: _____

   Dictionary definition: _____

   My meaning was: (Circle one)   correct   had correct parts   not close

3. He was known as a passionate and *charismatic* leader of the Shawnee people. (paragraph 7)

   I think *charismatic* means: _____

   Dictionary definition: _____

   My meaning was: (Circle one)   correct   had correct parts   not close

Tecumseh Word Search

```
A A I G Q S N K A B X F B V R R P X Y
A P R O C T O R E P U T A T I O N E Z
B B A O H E O I Q E P F R N B E N Q O
H X C P A C H D S Z B X T S M E L K O
V Q E R R U C L T F J W E Q S N P S T
I P Z F I M M P K N E I R S C G E U I
W Z Q U S S O M Z T U F H H J V N J C
H N I T M E X U L X K S C A N A D A E
W C Q G A H O N O R N F V W G L A G C
F U X K T B U D M J T F P N S I T A G
S K T V I U G V U S A H K E W A N I E
N S H K C V L P E V C P X E L N T H T
E K G W V P I O W X R Y W V B T H T F
G E L K S H R E W D O P O P S V S D I
J W M D A K J X N S N U D H B P O H K
```

Word Bank

barter

Canada

charismatic

honor

Proctor

reputation

Shawnee

shrewd

Tecumseh

valiant

Tecumseh Crossword

Across

2. a British Major General during the War of 1812

4. showing good judgment, intelligence and insight

5. following principles of good character

7. country to the north of the United States

9. a Native American nation of people

10. very influential or charming

Down

1. brave leader of the Shawnee nation

3. the view that is widely held about someone or something

6. to trade one thing for another

8. brave and loyal, even in defeat

Daniel Webster

"We the people of the United States, in Order to form a more perfect Union, establish Justice, insure domestic Tranquility, provide for the common defense, promote the general Welfare, and secure the Blessings of Liberty to ourselves and our Posterity, do ordain and establish this Constitution for the United States of America."

–Preamble to the United States Constitution

The Constitution is the foundation of our great nation. For one young boy who grew up on a small farm in New Hampshire, the constitution was the very heart of the country he loved so much. From the first time he read it, Daniel Webster never forgot its meaning. He cherished the words that his own father had fought for in the Revolutionary War. For the rest of his life, Daniel Webster would fight for the Constitution with his words, just as his father had fought with his hands.

Have you ever wondered how one document could last throughout our history? For more than 200 years, the Constitution has been the legs upon which this country has stood. There have been many people who have tried to change the Constitution to fit their own purposes. How is it then that this document has lasted over the years, untarnished? It was only with the help of people like Daniel Webster that our Constitution was not misconstrued or discarded as a compact between states instead of a document that was made:

"…for the people, by the people, and answerable to the people."

- Daniel Webster

Webster began his political career as a lawyer and public speaker. He graduated from Dartmouth College in 1801, already well-known on campus and around town for his oratory expertise. Daniel had an uncanny ability to memorize information quickly. This served him well as an orator and a lawyer.

Daniel started a law practice in Portsmouth, New Hampshire, where he quickly grew in popularity. At that time he married Grace Fletcher, who was a minister's daughter from his hometown of Salisbury. It was when Daniel represented the town of Portsmouth at a convention of people that it first became clear he was a strong leader. With mesmerizing speeches and a history of respectability, Daniel Webster won election to the House of Representatives in 1812, thus starting his life-long career in politics.

Being a popular lawyer, Daniel was able to make a substantial living from that profession. During his time, politicians did not make much money. Every time that Daniel Webster chose to serve his country as a congressman, a senator, and as Secretary of State, he and his family were sacrificing their life of comfort for a far less lavish alternative. Daniel was cherished by the people he represented in Congress. In fact, one year when his friends learned he would not be going back to Washington because of debt, they rallied together and honored his service to our country with a reception in New York and a large gift of money. With this kind of support Daniel had no choice but to continue serving.

One of the largest crowds ever to assemble in the senate chambers gathered to hear Daniel Webster declare, with unmatched conviction, the importance of the Constitution and the significance of unity. He spoke to preserve the Union above all else, without compromise. Some have called it one of the best orations ever given in the senate. These words were soon read around the world:

> *"Not a stripe erased or polluted, nor a single star obscured . . . but everywhere, spread all over in characters of living light, blazing on all its ample folds, as they float over the sea and over the land, and in every wind under the whole heavens, that other sentiment, dear to every true American heart—Liberty and Union, now and forever, one and inseparable!"*

> —Daniel Webster

The fight against the Constitution today might state that it is an outdated piece of history. But is the Constitution just as true today as it was over 200 years ago? What would Daniel Webster say to answer that question? Would you stand up for this document the way that he did? These are important questions that we might have to answer one day. My advice is to follow Daniel's lead. He made decisions that were not always popular, but because he felt they were right for the country, he overlooked his own popularity. Instead of having an allegiance to political leaders, or a specific political party, Daniel's allegiance was to his country. His legacy is as a defender of the Constitution and a patriot. His service to this country is truly immeasurable.

Discussion

Daniel Webster was famous for his devotion to the Constitution. This motivated him to do whatever he could to encourage others to protect the Union. As a result, in January of 1830 he ended up in a series of debates with Senator Robert Hayne of South Carolina. Senator Hayne was a strong defender of states' rights, and Senator Webster a strong defender of the Union of the States. This conflict would become one of the main causes of the Civil War. Talk with your teacher or parent about which principle he or she feels is more important and why. How do you think a compromise, or agreement where both sides accept a settlement that may be less than what was desired, is reached?

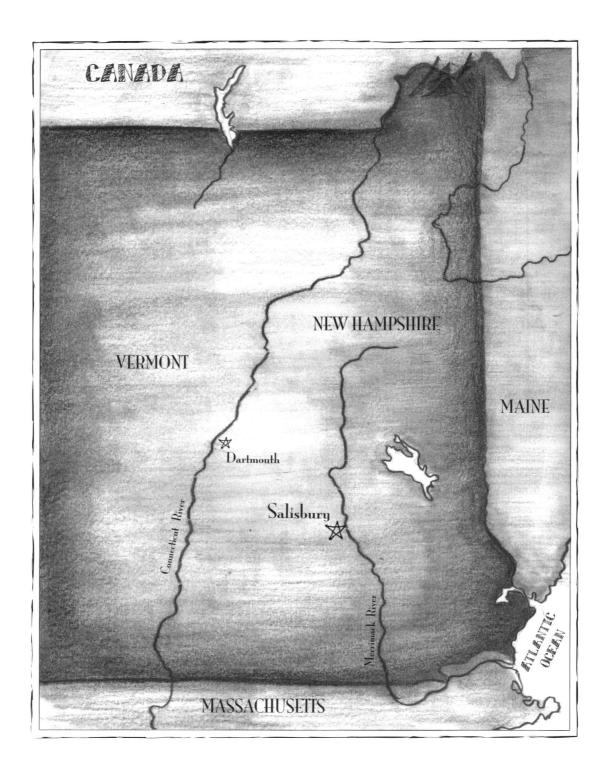

Timeline Review

Put things in perspective. Place Senator Daniel Webster's figure on the timeline in the year 1830, which was when he "replies to Hayne." Look at the other events before, during and after this year.

1828 — Andrew Jackson becomes our 7th president

1830 — Senator Daniel Webster "replies to Hayne"

1832 — Abraham Lincoln begins his political career

1836 — Texas becomes an independent territory

Activity

Read the Preamble to the Constitution and the Bill of Rights. Talk with your teacher or parent about what they say. Choose the amendment contained in the Bill of Rights that you think is most important. Come up with at least three reasons why you think it is the most important. Talk with others about the Bill of Rights and ask them to choose the amendment they think is most important. Debate, or discuss at length, your reasons. Can you come to a compromise, or agreement where both sides accept a settlement that may be less than what they wanted, on which amendment is most important?

Wordscramble

Here is a list of scrambled words that relate to the profile you read about Daniel Webster. Unscramble the letters and write the words correctly.

1. etebWeniaDlsr _____

2. ereetGrlhccaF _____

3. ortaro _____

4. socmpreiom _____

5. erSaton _____

6. mautrDhot _____

7. itotnsCtionu _____

8. ionnU _____

9. rdhceihes _____

10. icarscife _____

Using Context

Read the sentence and then look at the word in *italics*. Tell what you think that word means. Then look it up in a dictionary to confirm, or make sure of, the meaning. Tell someone about each word that you got correct. Remember, you will get better at understanding word meanings as you practice using context, or the words around a word.

1. He *cherished* the words that his own father had fought for in the Revolutionary War. (paragraph 2)

   I think *cherished* means: _____

   Dictionary definition: _____

   My meaning was: (Circle one)   correct   had correct parts   not close

2. With *mesmerizing* speeches and a history of respectability, Daniel Webster won election to the House of Representatives in 1812, thus starting his life-long career in politics. (paragraph 5)

   I think *mesmerizing* means: _____

   Dictionary definition: _____

   My meaning was: (Circle one)   correct   had correct parts   not close

3. He spoke to preserve the Union above all else, without compromise. (paragraph 7)

   I think *compromise* means: _____

   Dictionary definition: _____

   My meaning was: (Circle one)   correct   had correct parts   not close

Daniel Webster Word Search

```
E Z A L V D V W H T X L L J Q N T Y X
T S J P F A Q R A S E Q H I I K R J B
I N H C O N S T I T U T I O N H G P Q
Q Y U U N I O N H L Z G B G T R V J L
L V P R F E J T X N S S H B X S R T I
Z C V S C L A E C O M P R O M I S E L
T H U S U W S A C R I F I C E N U X Z
A E R L F E W I N A T G H L F Y I C I
N R C B R B P B C T A E U V D G C K Y
B I H R N S H I X O D H T D W L M R L
F S E N A T O R W R I W D S G T D E Q
N H D V I E B Z S K S N M K L R S H Z
D E D Z V R B S X S J Z J Q S C N T V
I D A R T M O U T H F M H A M C H Q Y
X N S V G R A C E F L E T C H E R L S
```

Word Bank

cherished

compromise

Constitution

Daniel Webster

Dartmouth

Grace Fletcher

orator

sacrifice

Senator

Union

Daniel Webster Crossword

Across

2. giving up something valuable
3. senator from New Hampshire
6. a skilled and persuasive speaker
7. something that is highly valued
9. another name for the United States of America
10. a settlement where both sides agree to less than what they wanted

Down

1. Webster's wife
4. the written document outlining the principles of American Government
5. University in Hanover, New Hampshire
8. an elected or appointed member of the Senate

Harriet Tubman

It was dark, cold, and she wasn't quite sure she was going in the right direction. It was the year 1849, and she was traveling by night so she wouldn't be caught. Back then, if you were black you were most likely not a free person, you were a slave. Harriet Tubman was born into slavery, but she knew that just because the color of your skin was different didn't mean that you should be treated any differently. So she decided to fight. She fought for freedom. She fought for her rights and for others like her. In the fall of 1849, Harriet traveled under the cover of darkness to her freedom. She went all the way from Maryland to Philadelphia on foot, guided by the North Star and various families that were connected to the Underground Railroad.

The Underground Railroad was a secret movement of brave families from the South all the way up into the North and Canada. They provided food and a safe place for runaway slaves to stay during their journey to freedom. Many of the people involved were white, although most were black. The Underground Railroad began near the end of the eighteenth century, and by the year 1850, the organization had sheltered and escorted around 100,000 fugitives to safety.

Harriet Tubman was a large part of that movement. She made many dangerous trips with the help of the Underground Railroad. She left her own comfort and liberty in the North to go all the way back to the perilous South, not just once but nineteen times to be exact. She knew full well that if she were caught, her fate would be death. Still she went. To her, helping others and saving them from a life of slavery was more important than her own safety. Of those trips, the first two were for her family members, but then her "passenger" list started to grow. Anyone who wanted a chance at freedom was well worth the effort. Altogether, Harriet Tubman saved over three hundred people from slavery, and miraculously, not one of them was ever lost or left behind. She wouldn't accept fear, and because of that she was not willing to let anyone turn back. This led to her reputation as the "Moses of her people."

Harriet never stopped fighting for what she believed in. When the Civil War began she did whatever was necessary to help the Union army. She was a nurse, a cook, and when needed she was an excellent spy due to the knowledge she gained from all of her covert, or secret, travels. She was even the first woman to lead an armed assault for the Union. Fear was a word that had no meaning for Harriet Tubman, and although she put herself in harm's way time and time again, she always escaped untouched. People started to say that she was "blessed of God" because of her amazing "luck."

After the war, Harriet made her home in Auburn, New York. She went on to open the John Brown Home for Aged and Indigent Colored People, as well as contribute her efforts to the fight for blacks to be able to vote. She lived a long life, and in 1913 yielded to her final sleep. Three hundred people owe her their freedom. Surely words cannot express the amount of time, effort, money, and giving of self that Harriet Tubman extended to our world. She showed us just what one person driven from within could accomplish.

Discussion

It says in the story that people felt Harriet Tubman had amazing "luck." Along with many other people in history who risked their lives for causes they believed in, she faced danger without hesitating because of the possible outcomes. After reading this story, talk with your teacher. Do you think Harriet Tubman's success was because of her good luck? If not, why do you think she and others in history were so successful?

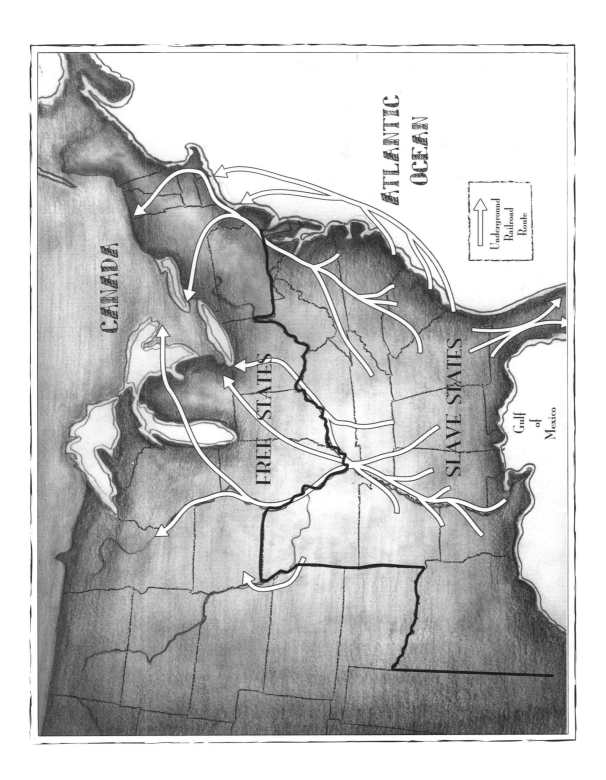

Timeline Review

Put things in perspective. Place Harriet Tubman's figure on the timeline in the year 1850, which was when she helped her first group of slaves to freedom. Look at the other events before, during, and after this year.

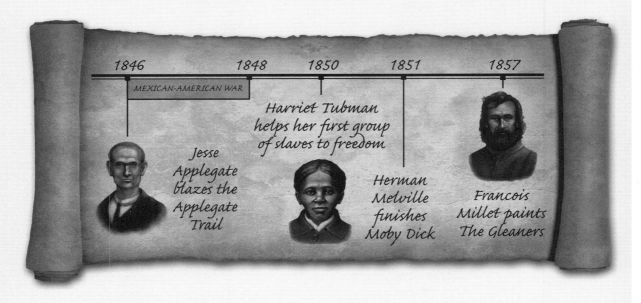

1846   1848   1850   1851   1857

MEXICAN-AMERICAN WAR

Harriet Tubman helps her first group of slaves to freedom

Jesse Applegate blazes the Applegate Trail

Herman Melville finishes Moby Dick

Francois Millet paints The Gleaners

Activity

The Underground Railroad was a network of those who were sympathetic or willing to help blacks escape from the bonds of slavery. In the South, there were severe consequences for those suspected of helping runaway slaves. What were those consequences? Learn more about the Underground Railroad. Where did it go, and how could fugitives recognize those who would help them? Once you have learned about it, talk with your teacher or parent about whether or not you would have wanted to be a part of this network. Tell why you would, or would not have wanted to participate.

Wordscramble

Here is a list of scrambled words that relate to the profile you read about Harriet Tubman. Unscramble the letters and write the words correctly.

1. lbtnaioiitso _____

2. uiHbTtanamerr _____

3. eUoRadudgonlanrridr _____

4. ysp _____

5. soMes _____

6. ilriivCaW _____

7. efvuigit _____

8. rimAnyUno _____

9. hortaSNtr _____

10. lvreysa _____

Before and After

Read the event on the left side and the event on the right side. Then decide if the first event (on the left) happened **before** or **after** the second event (on the right). Choose the word in the middle column that is correct. You may circle the correct answer or draw a line from the words *before* or *after* to the matching event.

1	Harriet Tubman was born a slave.	Before	After	The Civil War began.
2	Slavery was legal in the South.	Before	After	Harriet Tubman first escaped to the North.
3	The Civil War began.	Before	After	The Underground Railroad started.
4	Harriet escorted many people to freedom.	Before	After	The Civil War ended.
5	Harriet opened a home for old and poor blacks.	Before	After	Harriet served as a spy for the Union Army.

Harriet Tubman Word Search

```
A A I G Q S N K A B X F Z V R S P Y Y
A N O R T H S T A R R A I L R O A D Z
B B A A Y A O I Q E P F O N B E N Q O
H X C B X R M U N I O N A R M Y L K O
V Q E O X R O L T F J W D Q S N P S T
I P Z L C I S P K N E I G O C G E U I
W Z Q I B E E M Z T U F H A J E N J S
H N I T T T S U L X K S D R N K M Z L
W C Q I I T H B F G N F V C G B A G A
F U X O F U G I T I V E P Z S D T A V
S K T N J B G U N D E R G R O U N D E
N S H I H M L P E V C P X R L T T H R
E K G S V A I O W X R Y W V B Y H T Y
G E L T J N D I K I C I V I L W A R I
J W M D A K J X N S N U D H B P O H K
```

Word Bank

abolitionist

Civil War

fugitive

Harriet Tubman

Moses

North Star

slavery

spy

Underground Railroad

Union Army

Harriet Tubman Crossword

Across

3. former slave who led others to freedom
6. a network of those who helped fugitive slaves
9. someone asked by a government to get secret information
10. the Army of the United States, or the North

Down

1. requiring people to work by using force
2. a Biblical leader who led the Israelites out of slavery in Egypt
4. someone who is running away from captivity
5. the war between the North and the South
7. a bright star establishing direction for those who traveled by night
8. someone who spoke out against slavery

Thomas Jackson

Thomas Jackson was a famous General during the Civil War. He fought for the Confederacy. Many believed that if he hadn't died during the battle of Chancellorsville, the South might have won the war. No one knows for sure what would have happened, but when he died the South began to lose. What was it that made this General so influential?

The General himself would get down into the battle with his men and inspire them to do what they thought they could not. Because of that, Jackson and his men accomplished the impossible on more than one occasion. Fearlessly, he would stand with bullets flying past him and encourage his men to press onward. In the face of such leadership, how could they not follow him? His shrewd tactics and brilliant maneuvers are still being studied today. Once, when his Captain asked him how he could be so calm in the face of such danger, he said: "Captain, my religious belief teaches me to feel as safe in battle as in bed. God has fixed the time for my death. I do not concern myself about that, but to be always ready, no matter when it may overtake me. That is the way all men should live, and then all would be equally brave."

Thomas Jackson was only two years old when his father died, and was seven when he became an orphan. Growing up wasn't easy for this young boy. Since he moved around so much throughout his childhood, he was mostly self-taught. Never a very talented student, he made up for what he didn't know with hard work. Hard work would soon become something that governed Jackson's life. When he was about eighteen years old a local congressman announced that there was an opening in the military academy at West Point. So Jackson and three other boys applied. Unfortunately, Jackson did not get the appointment but as fate would have it, the boy who did decided West Point was not for him. Therefore, off Jackson went to the military academy. It was perfect for him—hard work, rules, everything he valued. Jackson once said, "A man of words and not of deeds is like a garden full of weeds." He also had to work extra hard to keep up in his classes, but managed to move up from the bottom of his class during his first year, all the way to seventeenth out of fifty-nine students in his graduating year.

After graduation, he served in the Army during the Mexican-American War for a short time. Then, he became a professor at the Virginia Military Institute. During this time his life was met with more tragedy. After a short marriage his wife died during childbirth, along with their newborn baby. But happiness did not elude him forever. He remarried three years later, and from the many letters written to his dearest "Anna" during the war, we can assume that they were very happy together. It was during the 1860 election, when Abraham Lincoln became president, that Jackson knew war was eminent. In April of 1861 he assembled his famous brigade, and so began one of the most remarkable military ventures in history.

On the way to their first real battle, Jackson's brigade was leading the Shenandoah Army in a march to meet the others. Since the men hadn't really seen war yet, they had never seen their leader truly lead. They weren't marching with the kind of determination that Jackson expected from his men, so he stopped them. In a loud, stern voice he read from an official statement, "Our gallant army under General Beauregard is now attacked by overwhelming numbers." He then said, "Step out like men and make a forced march to save the country." They did step up. They quickened their pace, marched through pain, waded through a river, and after eighteen long hours they arrived at Bull Run, the first important battle of the Civil War.

From what they could tell, the battle was not going their way. Confederates were scrambling and retreating, but Jackson wasn't ready to give up yet. They hadn't come all that way for nothing. He rallied his men and while others were falling back, he stood without hesitation, without fear amidst the bullets and the enemy's threats. One general who was desperately trying to get his men to hold their positions said to them "There's Jackson standing like a stone wall! Rally behind the Virginians!" The men on the battlefield started taking notice of this man who seemed to have no fear. Through his bravery, they became brave, and it was the beginning of a turning point in the battle. The South won that day. Afterward, he became known as "Stonewall" Jackson, and the name never left him. His men also were called "the Stonewall Brigade," a name they carried with great pride.

Though Stonewall Jackson fought for the South and his home state of Virginia, he was not necessarily for slavery. Nor was he against it. He had slaves of his own but he believed that they deserved fair and humane treatment. He even started the first Sunday school for slaves where he lived. He wasn't fighting a war so that people could have slaves. He was fighting so that states could decide for themselves. He believed that it was not the government's place to tell the states what they could or could not do.

Jackson's troops chanted his name as they charged into battle. They knew that just the power of his name would send terror into the hearts of their enemy. They were proud of their leader and the reputation he had given them. Even his prisoners boasted that the great Stonewall had captured them. But it wasn't just the victories they were proud of. When they suffered, he suffered. The troops knew that as they slept short hours on the cold, hard, ground, so did he. He never took advantage of his position.

After an attack in which Stonewall forced a retreat on two very capable adversaries, General Freemont and General Shields, he said, "He who does not see the hand of God in this is blind, sir, blind!" Stonewall's faith was so important to him that after every victory he would kneel in his tent and give thanks to God. He was known for his unconventional ways. During his last battle, when he received a mortal wound, he and General Lee came up with the most brilliant plan of his career. The South needed a clever and unexpected strategy to get out of a bad situation, so General Lee and General Jackson thought, discussed, and finally decided. Jackson would take his men down a small back road behind the cover of woods and surprise the enemy. They never expected him, and even though the Confederates were outnumbered and starting from a bad position, they succeeded. This was, of course, what Stonewall loved the most—doing the impossible!

It was during this excursion that a few men made a very terrible mistake. During the night, Stonewall went to inspect their circumstances when a group of men opened fire. They thought Jackson and the men he led were enemies—a mistake that I'm sure they regretted for the rest of their lives. Though injured to the point where they had to amputate his left arm, it seemed as though Jackson was on the mend. Then he developed pneumonia, and on Sunday May 10, 1863, he breathed his last. "It is the Lord's Day; my wish is fulfilled. I have always desired to die on Sunday," Jackson told his wife Anna. The night Jackson died, General Lee said to his cook, "William, I have lost my right arm," and "I'm bleeding at the heart."

What is the mark of a great man? Integrity? Leadership? Bravery? What about having a group of men who respect you so much that they will risk their very lives at just a word? Some of the survivors from the Stonewall Brigade had such loyalty to their leader that years after the war ended, during a reunion, they chose to sleep on the ground around a statue of Jackson in Richmond, Virginia. One of them said, "We were his boys, and we wanted to sleep with the Old Man just once more." To me, *this* is the mark of a great man. Stonewall's legacy is so much more than just what he did. It is who he was.

Discussion

There are examples through history of leaders who inspire men to do things in battle that are both dangerous and heroic. During the Civil War in the South, Stonewall Jackson and Robert E. Lee were such leaders. For the North, Abraham Lincoln and Joshua Chamberlain were also this type of leader. After reading the profile on Joshua Chamberlain, talk with your teacher or parent about the ways that these two soldiers were different and the ways that they were the same, in their personal lives and as military men.

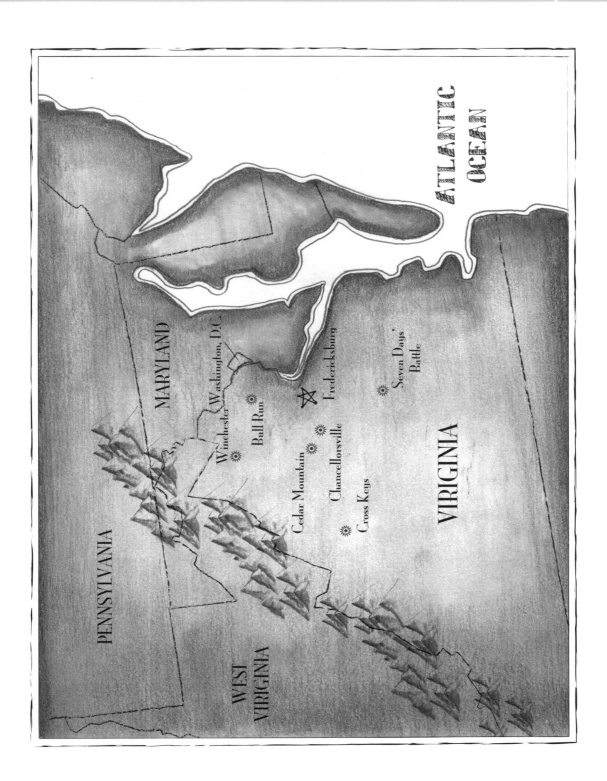

Timeline Review

Put things in perspective. Place Thomas Jackson's figure on the timeline in the year 1861 which was when he became "Stonewall" Jackson. Look at the other events before, during, and after this year.

Activity

Monuments, or structures designed to pay tribute to a person or people, are located throughout the world. Many monuments exist to honor those who have given their lives in service to their community, state, or country. This could have happened during times of war or over the course of time. Do some research and find out if there are any monuments in your town. If so, visit the monument and learn about it. Do you think it is a fitting, or appropriate, honor? Choose someone you know or someone you have read about in this book and design a monument to that person.

Wordscramble

Here is a list of scrambled words that relate to the profile you read about Thomas Jackson. Unscramble the letters and write the words correctly.

1. awloleStrgaineBd _____

2. mToosJshkncaa _____

3. REeteLebor _____

4. oraltm _____

5. uoaRtefBulltBln _____

6. ginriiVa _____

7. PensittWo _____

8. eriaehlpsd _____

9. yoyltla _____

10. segyrtat _____

Using Context

Read the sentence and then look at the word in *italics*. Tell what you think that word means. Then look it up in a dictionary to confirm, or make sure of, the meaning. Tell someone about each word that you got correct. Remember, you will get better at understanding word meanings as you practice using context, or the words around a word.

1. In the face of such *leadership*, how could they not follow him? (paragraph 2)

   I think *leadership* means: _____

   Dictionary definition: _____

   My meaning was: (Circle one)   correct   had correct parts   not close

2. During his last battle, when he received a *mortal* wound, he and General Lee came up with the most brilliant plan of his career. (paragraph 9)

   I think *mortal* means: _____

   Dictionary definition: _____

   My meaning was: (Circle one)   correct   had correct parts   not close

3. Some of the survivors from the Stonewall Brigade had such *loyalty* to their leader that years after the war ended, during a reunion, they chose to sleep on the ground around a statue of Jackson in Richmond, Virginia. (paragraph 11)

   I think *loyalty* means: _____

   Dictionary definition: _____

   My meaning was: (Circle one)   correct   had correct parts   not close

Thomas Jackson Word Search

```
V  S  T  O  N  E  W  A  L  L  B  R  I  G  A  D  E  U  L
F  Z  R  O  B  E  R  T  E  L  E  E  Q  I  M  G  P  U  E
V  O  T  S  G  K  Q  X  L  P  H  D  S  V  X  F  U  K  A
B  Q  L  T  C  K  U  G  Q  T  U  M  W  Y  C  G  R  M  D
I  I  W  R  A  S  L  W  E  S  T  P  O  I  N  T  B  O  E
J  R  F  A  S  Y  R  Y  V  I  R  G  I  N  I  A  E  V  R
B  A  T  T  L  E  O  F  B  U  L  L  R  U  N  A  K  M  S
Z  U  Q  E  F  S  M  C  T  J  H  I  A  U  I  F  V  C  H
I  S  B  G  I  S  M  V  M  O  R  T  A  L  L  F  Y  G  I
Z  Z  Q  Y  B  O  U  I  O  C  R  X  P  O  R  Z  E  A  P
H  U  Q  T  H  O  M  A  S  J  A  C  K  S  O  N  P  B  O
T  I  Y  Q  C  E  T  G  N  P  S  W  C  E  T  J  Y  Q  F
B  H  H  S  D  S  B  X  J  E  C  T  F  E  T  N  H  Q  I
U  R  R  C  F  I  Y  X  A  W  L  O  Y  A  L  T  Y  O  S
U  Z  R  Z  L  O  U  L  Z  B  M  U  D  X  A  P  F  V  S
```

Word Bank

Battle of Bull Run

leadership

loyalty

mortal

Robert E. Lee

Stonewall Brigade

strategy

Thomas Jackson

Virginia

West Point

Thomas Jackson Crossword

Across

3. the ability to lead or guide people
4. the home state of Thomas Jackson
7. known as "Stonewall," a great strategist for the Confederate Army
9. the United States Army Military Academy

Down

1. Union name for the First Battle of Manassas
2. the brigade under the command of Thomas Jackson
3. an attitude of duty and devotion to a person or cause
5. commander of the Confederate forces
6. leading to death, such as a mortal wound
8. a carefully thought out plan of action

Clara Barton

Have you ever been in a situation where you saw someone in need of help and you were torn because you didn't feel like helping? Sure, many of us have had that feeling before. Maybe this happened to you, or someone you know. Perhaps someone needed help with a broken down car on the side of the road, or maybe you passed by a needy person but didn't have the time to stop. We always reassure ourselves by saying someone else will come along and do what we couldn't. For Clara Barton, that was a thought she couldn't accept.

Clara can only be described as strong, intelligent, sympathetic, compassionate, merciful, and nurturing. Whoever was sick would be cared for, and whoever was in need would be helped. She had a true gift of caring for others, and she used this gift throughout her life to affect the lives of many. Most only know Clara as the founder of the Red Cross in America. Let me introduce you to another side of her that many people don't know.

Clara was born on a wintry Christmas day in North Oxford, Massachusetts. Her family lived there on a farm. Clara learned many things from her family, and first realized her love of caring for others when her brother David was badly injured. She was a young girl, not more than eleven at the time, yet she rarely left her brother's side while caring for him. Gratefully, he recovered after about two years. Clara also learned from her father, who she watched with pride as he generously gave to the community in many ways. Though she was timid as a girl, Clara would eventually become braver than most of the grown men she knew.

At the age of seventeen Clara became a teacher at a local school near North Oxford. She soon found that she was very good at creating order and enjoyed finding new ways to interest her students in learning. Teaching was not just a profession for Clara. She used it to help children who either couldn't afford to pay for school, or didn't even have a school to go to. Clara started a free school in New Jersey, where she convinced the townspeople that if they gave her a building she would teach their children without pay. For Clara it was about the students, not the money.

Clara was living in Washington, D.C., and working as a clerk at the patent office when the Civil War broke out. Every decision and every circumstance in Clara's life had led her to this place, at this time. Her big heart gave her the courage she needed to put her own well-being aside and change the futures of many wounded soldiers over the next few years.

She began by sending a letter to her home state, after seeing the poor condition of a regiment that arrived in Washington from Massachusetts, asking for any help the state could offer to these lonely, beat up boys. On their way to the Capital, the regiment had been robbed and battered by townspeople who opposed the Union Army. To her surprise the letter drew a huge response. Clara did all she could to give these men hope.

As the war continued, Clara kept gathering supplies and helping whom she could, but helping from a distance was not enough for her. She needed to do more. She knew that the time between injury and arrival at the hospital was too great. Men who could have lived, were dying simply because they weren't being treated soon enough. But what could she do? Women were not allowed at the front. The idea had entered Clara's mind though, and she couldn't get it out. So she fought for the opportunity to help right on the battlefields. She eventually convinced a Major that she could handle the dangers and the horrors of battle. Not only would Clara care for their injuries, she would talk to them, read to them, and even write letters to their families for them. It was these kinds of things that strengthened their spirits, not just their bodies. The men did need a woman's touch, though many women would have fainted, wept, or become hysterical at the things Clara saw and experienced. She was able to deal with the distressing situations only because she knew that if she couldn't control her emotions, she would be of no help to the wounded men.

There's no way to know just how many lives Clara Barton saved. She was a great organizer, and when she saw a need she organized people and supplies in such a way that it optimized their capacity. For the lives that Clara couldn't save, she would ease their suffering as best she could. There has been more than one story told of soldiers who, in their near death and delirious state, recognized Clara to be their mother, sister, or someone else they loved. Knowing their time was limited, Clara would speak to them as the voice they wanted to hear, always comforting, always reassuring. It was not long before she gained a reputation as "The Angel of the Battlefield." In a letter to her father Clara wrote: "I may be compelled to face danger, but never fear it, and while our soldiers can stand and fight, I can stand and feed and nurse them."

The next time you notice someone in need, think of Clara. Do as she would have done. Do it in honor of a woman who dedicated her life to serving others. The word "selfish" had no meaning to Clara Barton, who could never put her own desires above someone else's needs. So now that you know about her, take a piece of Clara with you wherever you go.

Discussion

Following the Civil War, Clara spent time working to identify those who had died and their burial sites. She felt that this was important because it brought comfort and closure to the families. Abraham Lincoln sent a letter to Clara, honoring her work. While others may have felt that this was not important work since the soldiers were already dead, to Clara it was very important to help families and honor the memories of the soldiers. Read more about the Tomb of the Unknown Soldier at Arlington National Cemetery. This is one way our country can honor fallen soldiers who have died without identification. Tell why you think this is important to the families of soldiers who have died.

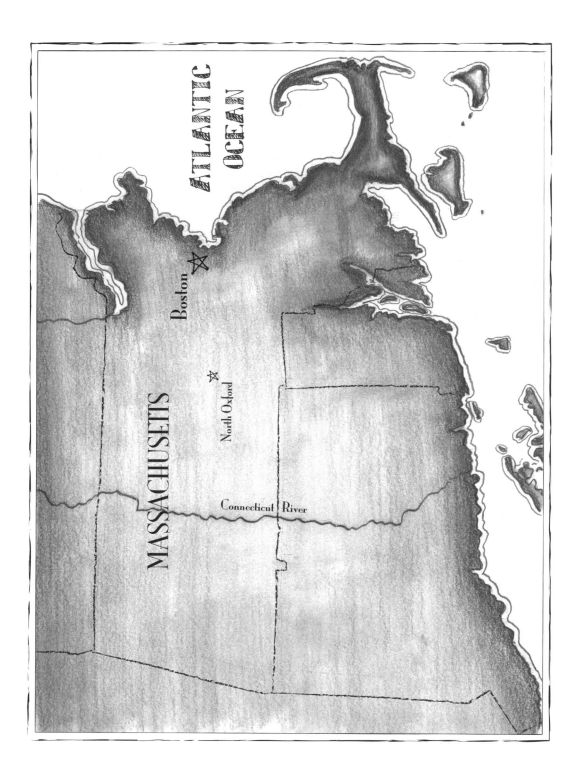

Timeline Review

Put things in perspective. Place Clara Barton's figure on the timeline in the year 1862, which was when she became known as "The Angel of the Battlefield." Look at the other events before, during, and after this year.

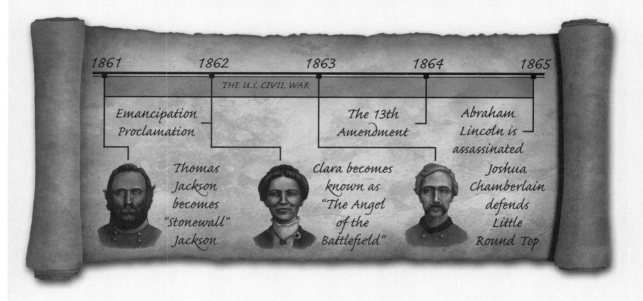

THE U.S. CIVIL WAR

1861 — 1862 — 1863 — 1864 — 1865

Emancipation Proclamation

The 13th Amendment

Abraham Lincoln is assassinated

Thomas Jackson becomes "Stonewall" Jackson

Clara becomes known as "The Angel of the Battlefield"

Joshua Chamberlain defends Little Round Top

Activity

The Red Cross in America has become synonymous, or one and the same, with hope and help for the suffering. This is true not only during wartime, but also in the event of earthquakes, storms, and all kinds of natural disasters. Learn more about the American Red Cross. Is there a branch of the Red Cross in your community? It depends on donations and volunteers to help the needy. With your parents' permission, contact the Red Cross in your area and find out what their needs are and what services they provide.

Wordscramble

Here is a list of scrambled words that relate to the profile you read about Clara Barton. Unscramble the letters and write the words correctly.

1. lCtaBoarrna _____

2. xrhNtrfOdoo _____

3. eglBttlendAaielf _____

4. isnacoomps _____

5. rmyce _____

6. egacuro _____

7. nyomiUrAn _____

8. nesur _____

9. noDnCitasWhg _____

10. podiietzm _____

Using Context

Read the sentence and then look at the word in *italics*. Tell what you think that word means. Then look it up in a dictionary to confirm, or make sure of, the meaning. Tell someone about each word that you got correct. Remember, you will get better at understanding word meanings as you practice using context, or the words around a word.

1. Clara can only be described as strong, intelligent, sympathetic, *compassionate*, merciful, and nurturing. (paragraph 2)

   I think *compassionate* means: _____

   Dictionary definition: _____

   My meaning was: (Circle one)   correct   had correct parts   not close

2. Her big heart gave her the *courage* she needed to put her own well being aside and change the futures of many wounded soldiers over the next few years. (paragraph 5)

   I think *courage* means: _____

   Dictionary definition: _____

   My meaning was: (Circle one)   correct   had correct parts   not close

3. She was a great organizer, and when she saw a need she organized people and supplies in such a way that it *optimized* their capacity. (paragraph 8)

   I think *optimized* means: _____

   Dictionary definition: _____

   My meaning was: (Circle one)   correct   had correct parts   not close

Clara Barton Word Search

```
S M B A T T L E F I E L D A N G E L D
K S H L N B V R W D S F N M J A A C H
S M Y C C O M P A S S I O N H Y Q N N
T S R Z L P W A S X J A R O T A T C B
R P R R A T H T H M I M T R C A W I W
O R M R R I V A I I C O H E O W M Z M
D Y M T A M B F N Y Y K O Z U A W N G
M F D Y B I R Y G R R H X M R G H Z M
N E M S A Z S S T M M O F V A D X S S
Y F Q C R E D L O K S W O O G J V P J
T P J E T D W Q N I W M R T E U W K V
W L I E O T L B D S A W D G A S B L B
R Z S I N O V B C M E R C Y Q X A L M
S B H M D A B P J U N I O N A R M Y X
S H D B T W G R P N U R S E L S B G T
```

Word Bank

Battlefield Angel
Clara Barton
compassion
courage
mercy

North Oxford
nurse
optimized
Union Army
Washington, D. C.

Clara Barton Crossword

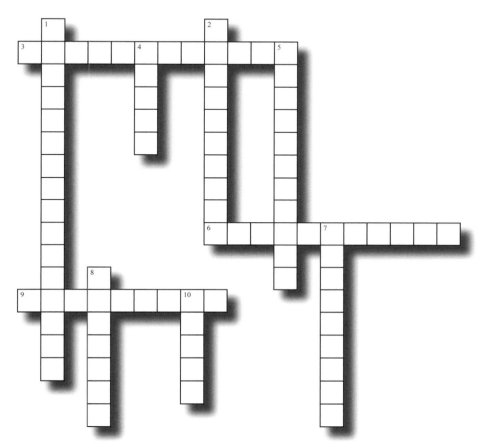

Across

3. national capital, Clara's home for a time
6. Clara's birthplace in Massachusetts
9. name of the northern troops who opposed the Confederates in the Civil War

Down

1. the name given Clara Barton by troops she assisted
2. concern for, and a desire to relieve the suffering of, others
4. someone trained to care for the sick and injured
5. founder of the American Red Cross
7. made something work the best that it could
8. the ability to face difficulty, pain, or danger without fear or giving up
10. compassion shown to others

Joshua Chamberlain

Joshua Chamberlain was a visionary. As such, he was able to see the big picture in many situations. He could often see exactly what changes should be made. That is why Joshua Chamberlain was a great leader. He led a classroom when he was a professor at Bowdoin College in Maine, led the Twentieth Maine Regiment in the Civil War, led the entire state of Maine four times as Governor, and led Bowdoin College when he became its President in 1871. Joshua Chamberlain was born to be a leader, and a great one at that. He was a man of integrity, ideals, patriotism, and vision.

Chamberlain was born near the town of Brewer, Maine, in 1828. He was the oldest of five children born to hard-working, successful parents. Gifted academically, in 1848 he started attending Bowdoin College and met his future wife, Fannie Adams, while there. Together they would have five children, and remain happily married until Fannie's death in 1905. Before the outbreak of the Civil War, Joshua was a professor at his Alma Mater. However, the beginning of the war meant change for him as he answered duty's call to serve his country.

During the battle of Gettysburg, which was later viewed as the turning point of the Civil War, Joshua Chamberlain played a key role. Many things had to fall into place at that battle for the Union Army to have victory. If the South had not been defeated, they might have won the war. Ironically, the battle was decided on July 3rd, the day before America celebrates its freedom.

Joshua's part started before the battle even began. A group of displaced soldiers and mutineers from another Maine regiment were sent to him to either make fight, or to dispose of, but Joshua saw the bigger picture. He knew the importance of the coming battles, and that even one man could make the difference between victory and defeat. Therefore, with the kind of inspiration that can only come from conviction, Joshua Chamberlain aroused honor from the hearts of those men, and all but a handful rejoined the Union Army.

Next, the Twentieth Maine traveled to take part in the epic battle at Gettysburg. Their directive was to defend the extreme left flank of the Union's army. They were ordered to hold no matter the circumstance. So when the regiment had used all their ammunition after defending against many waves of Confederate soldiers, most commanders would have had no choice but to retreat. This was not an option that Joshua Chamberlain accepted. He did the only thing that could have saved them. He ordered his men to fix bayonets and charge! The Confederate soldiers were so shocked by the Union's audacity that they surrendered, even though they still had shots left in their muskets. Joshua Chamberlain's actions that day earned him the Congressional Medal of Honor.

Without Chamberlain's speech to a group of seemingly useless soldiers, the Twentieth Maine would most likely not have been able to keep their hold of Little Round Top. Without holding Little Round Top, the Union Army might have lost the battle at Gettysburg. Without having victory at Gettysburg, the Union might have lost the war.

During the Civil War, many of the people who fought against each other were friends, neighbors, brothers, from the same town or state. Oftentimes it was through painful turmoil that these men met on the battlefields. Joshua Chamberlain fought for the freedom of all men. He fought to preserve the Union. He recognized though, that many of his "enemies" were doing what they thought to be right. They were trying to defend their homes and their way of life. Many of them were admirable men, who fought bravely and fiercely. His respect paved the way for yet another honor.

Selected at war's end, Joshua Chamberlain received the surrender of the Army of Northern Virginia. I can't imagine what treatment the Confederate soldiers and their leaders expected that day. In their wildest imaginings, I know they didn't think it would be with respect. Joshua's integrity enabled him to show mercy to the defeated soldiers. As they were marching toward the Union Army, Chamberlain, followed by his men, saluted the surrendering soldiers of the South.

A monument stands at Gettysburg in dedication to Chamberlain, the Twentieth Maine, and what they did for this country. On the day of its dedication, Joshua Chamberlain said this in a speech of the hallowed ground on which so many men gave their lives:

> *"In great deeds something abides. On great fields something stays. Forms change and pass; bodies disappear; but spirits linger, to consecrate ground for the vision-place of souls. And reverent men and women from afar, and generations that know us not and that we know not of, heart-drawn to see where and by whom great things were suffered and done for them, shall come to this deathless field to ponder and dream; and lo! the shadow of a mighty presence shall wrap them in its bosom, and the power of the vision pass into their souls."*

Discussion

Joshua Chamberlain's personal conviction of giving his life if necessary directed him as a leader, yet he respected those who fought for the other side. His belief in the importance of the restored Union may have directed him to treat his opponents fairly, hoping that one day there would be unity in the nation once again. This was a difficult thing to do since so many people held their beliefs so strongly, including Chamberlain. Do you think Chamberlain's example was a good one? What affect do you think this treatment had on the soldiers in the Confederate Army? Do you think things would have been different if others had followed his example throughout the Northern and Southern states?

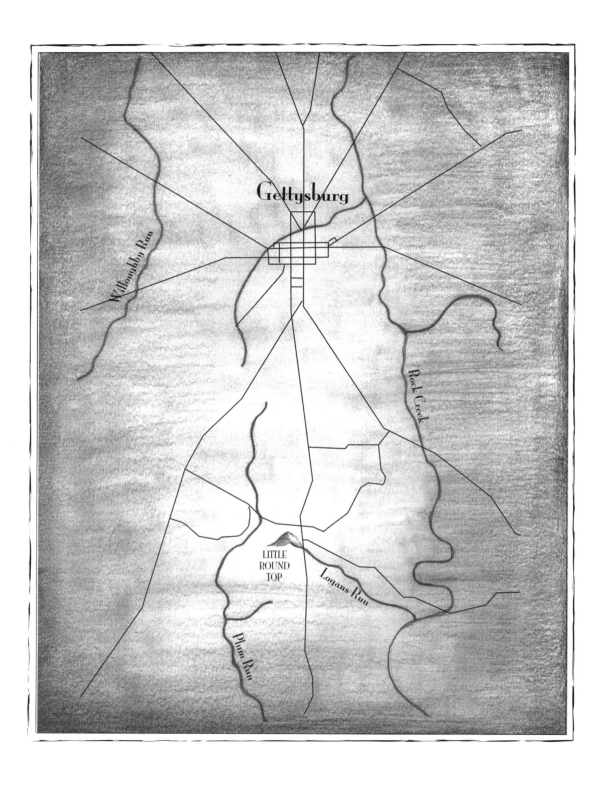

Timeline Review

Put things in perspective. Place Joshua Chamberlain's figure on the timeline in the year 1863, which was when he defended Little Round Top. Look at the other events before, during, and after this year.

Activity

The battle of Gettysburg was a key battle, helping to determine the outcome of the Civil War. The job given to Joshua Chamberlain in this battle was extremely difficult. He was to hold a position in the foothills named Little Round Top. This position was the end of the Union line, and as such was vulnerable to the enemy. Learn more about the Battle of Gettysburg, and in particular Little Round Top. Draw a diagram that shows what happened that day. Use blue pencils or markers to show the Union position, and red to show the position of the Confederate army. Can you think of any moves you would have tried if you had commanded the Confederate army?

Wordscramble

Here is a list of scrambled words that relate to the profile you read about Joshua Chamberlain. Unscramble the letters and write the words correctly.

1. ahiCJholremaansbu _____

2. inneAsmdaaF _____

3. ooColdewBgilne _____

4. oGrerovn _____

5. sporrfsoe _____

6. WiliravC _____

7. tenTiMeenhiatw _____

8. redeal _____

9. hoonr _____

10. uesGrbgtty _____

Before and After

Read the event on the left side and the event on the right side. Then decide if the first event (on the left) happened **before** or **after** the second event (on the right). Choose the word in the middle column that is correct. You may circle the correct answer or draw a line from the words *before* or *after* to the matching event.

1	Joshua Chamberlain was a professor at Bowdoin College.	Before	After	The Civil War began.
2	Chamberlain led his troops at the Battle of Gettysburg.	Before	After	Chamberlain convinced members of the Second Maine to rejoin the fight.
3	Chamberlain's troops successfully held Little Round Top.	Before	After	Chamberlain's troops ran out of bullets and charged the enemy.
4	The Civil War ended.	Before	After	Chamberlain received the surrender of the Confederate soldiers.
5	Chamberlain was elected Governor of Maine.	Before	After	He was a hero at the Battle of Gettysburg.

Joshua Chamberlain Word Search

```
Y G L I K I X N E O I L U Y B I U T R
S H O N O R H E X T X B N I T S K W K
O C Y C R E L U Z R D N X H M G B E U
J C J L J L M T D B I X M M E H G N T
G O V E R N O R O P V P M X U I R T U
S Q A A O T G C X W B N B B C B X I A
B O W D O I N C O L L E G E I Y X E X
I G G E T T Y S B U R G L D V C R T V
G H E R J E V J Y K L H L R I R V H V
R J N D L P M A D W I W Q Z L F A M C
D T Y A B F M E U T F I Z J W C P A B
J O S H U A C H A M B E R L A I N I O
V B X Y T B P R O F E S S O R I C N C
F A N N I E A D A M S Z D L Q U D E P
R G C M B D Y M U L I J I E A Y P I R
```

Word Bank

Bowdoin College

Civil War

Fannie Adams

Gettysburg

Governor

honor

Joshua Chamberlain

leader

professor

Twentieth Maine

Joshua Chamberlain Crossword

Across

2. a post held in Maine by Chamberlain four times

3. regiment led by Colonel Chamberlain

6. Union Colonel who won a great victory at Gettysburg

7. site in Pennsylvania of key Civil War battle

9. college in Maine attended by Chamberlain

Down

2. a teacher of the highest rank at a college or university

4. the war fought between forces from the Union and Confederacy

5. Colonel Chamberlain's wife

8. strong moral character and personal dignity

10. someone who guides others by example

Booker T. Washington

The year was 1865, and the Civil War had just ended. The Union Army defeated the Confederates. All slaves were now free. The day they had hoped and prayed for had finally come. Women wept, men shouted for joy and children, such as one by the name of Booker T. Washington, didn't understand completely—but he knew that something very important had just happened.

Although fierce fighting won freedom for them, the former slaves of America now had to find their place in society. Many of them even decided to stay with the families they had grown up serving. For some it was out of loyalty, love, and friendship that they decided to stay. For others, it was because they didn't know what else to do. Slavery was all they had known their whole lives. Though horrible, demoralizing, and painful, it was still all they knew. Most slaves did not go to school or know how to read. So after the war ended, they had no other life to turn to, no skills, nothing other than what they were forced to do as slaves.

Imagine that from about the time you could walk, you worked doing hard labor. No school and no self worth, only work. This was the case for young Booker. The only way to truly empathize with him is to picture yourself as this little boy, born into a world that was fighting desperately to hold him down. Many of his peers accepted this fate. They gave in to injustice, and it certainly was the easier road to take, but not for Booker. He would never give in and never back down. He devoted his life to fighting the uphill battles. He knew that he was fighting for something much bigger than he was. He was fighting for justice. Would you have had the strength? Would you have endured the persecution and the maltreatment, all the while knowing that just giving up would bring relief? Booker's determination changed countless lives. He knew that the road less traveled was always the one worth the effort. He would never have been happy any other way.

From a very young age, Booker had an insatiable desire to learn. He even taught himself to read because of this desire. When the small West Virginia town his family lived in started a school, he worked his normal, exhausting amount of hours before and after his classes so that he could attend. His mother, who loved him dearly, would have gladly sent him to school free from the burden of work, but with rent and other mouths to feed, she was left without a choice.

One day when Booker overheard some men talking about a college for colored people called Hampton Institute in Virginia, he knew that he had stumbled upon his destiny. Hampton taught its students requiring no tuition from them, only that they work for their education. This suited Booker, as he had no money to give and valued hard work above little else. Through perseverance, Booker T. Washington grasped at this chance for change. He did whatever was necessary to attend Hampton, unwilling to accept anything less than his goal.

The principal of Hampton was a man by the name of Samuel Armstrong. He was an accomplished general during the Civil War for the Union Army. He became Booker's role model, and their relationship was an important part of shaping his future. The experience at Hampton left a deep impression on Booker's life. Upon graduating, he would become everything that his mentor, General Armstrong, had hoped for and much more. When he returned to his hometown of Malden, West Virginia, Booker started imparting what he had learned to others. He taught classes throughout the week, as well as night classes, and even Sunday classes. Booker remembered his days of trying to find time for school and wanted to make sure that everyone had the opportunity to attend.

After striving for a couple of years to influence the community of Malden, Booker was invited to be a teacher back at his Alma Mater, Hampton. He was thrilled and honored to accept the position. It was through this opportunity that an even more important one came. General Armstrong recommended Booker to head a new school for blacks opening in Tuskegee, Alabama. Knowing the significance of this prospect,

Booker was eager to accept. From Hampton, he took with him all the knowledge and determination necessary to make an impact on the small town of Tuskegee forevermore.

I wonder if the thirty students who came to Booker's first class, held in a leaky church building, knew what they were getting themselves into. Booker not only taught academic knowledge, he taught discipline, cleanliness, faith, and integrity. He also made a point to prepare his students for a professional future by giving them different kinds of industrial training. I also wonder if Booker knew that from those meager beginnings would come a school of 1,500 students and 100 buildings, built with the students' own hands. Through his school at Tuskegee, Booker's dreams came true. It produced men and women who were independent, skilled, and disciplined, who would turn around and use their knowledge to influence the communities around them.

Tuskegee attracted men of character such as George Washington Carver, who led the agricultural science department. He taught there for 47 years, and greatly improved agriculture in the South. The school became Tuskegee University in 1985, with 3,000 students attending and a continuing reputation of quality.

There was something uncommon about the way that Booker T. Washington lived. He required excellence of himself, overcame insurmountable odds, and inspired thousands to do the same. Booker encouraged the men and women who shared in his unjust and unimaginable childhood to forgive those who had enslaved them. He knew that bitterness and hatred would only hold them back. In his profound wisdom he said this of hatred:

> *"I will permit no man to narrow and degrade my soul by making me hate him."*

In 1895, at the Cotton States and International Exhibition in Atlanta, Booker gave a speech that catapulted him into nationwide recognition. He spoke inspiringly on the importance of the two races working together. He appealed with gracious and humble eloquence to the thousands of blacks and whites who had gathered. Booker gave many stirring speeches over the years, and he wrote numerous articles addressing the issues of his day. In 1900, he founded the National Negro Business League to support black businesses. In 1901 his autobiography, *Up From Slavery,* was published.

He was the first African American to have tea with the Queen of England, dinner with the President of the United States, and the first to receive an honorary degree from Harvard. By the year 1915, Booker T. Washington had given all he had to give. With his health rapidly deteriorating, Booker realized that the end was near after delivering what would be his final speech in New York City. He was determined to hold on long enough to make it back home to Tuskegee. After only hours of reaching his destination, he let go of the life during which he had accomplished so much, but which had taken much out of him. Booker was only fifty-nine when he passed away. Over 8,000 people honored his life at his funeral, and countless others around the country mourned their loss. He was undeniably one of the most influential African Americans of his time. His legacy spread all over the globe, and generation upon generation have gained much wisdom from his tremendous leadership. Still he points back to the key to his success and character:

> *"I have learned that success is to be measured not so much by the position that one has reached in life as by the obstacles which he has overcome while trying to succeed."*

- Booker T. Washington

Discussion

After experiencing the pain of slavery, it would be quite understandable for people to react with hatred towards those who had mistreated them. Though understandable, hatred is not beneficial or helpful to those who suffered, or to those around them trying to build new lives. Reread the following quote by Booker T. Washington:

> *"I will permit no man to narrow and degrade my soul by making me hate him."*

Do you think this is difficult to do? Talk with your teacher or parent about Booker's circumstances growing up. Do you think he had opportunity to hate others? Do you know anyone who has suffered in some way and feels angry about it? Do you think Booker's words and story would help that person?

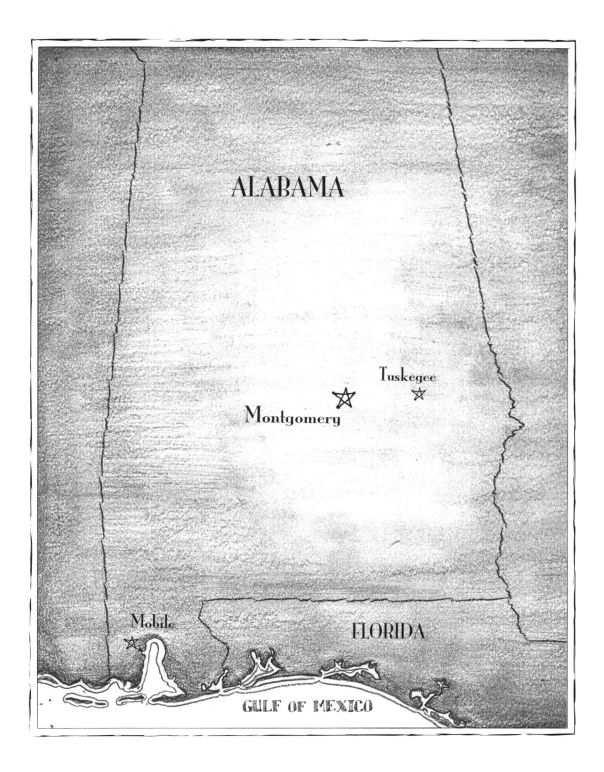

Timeline Review

Put things in perspective. Place Booker T. Washington's figure on the timeline in the year 1881, which was when he opened the Tuskagee Institute. Look at the other events before, during, and after this year

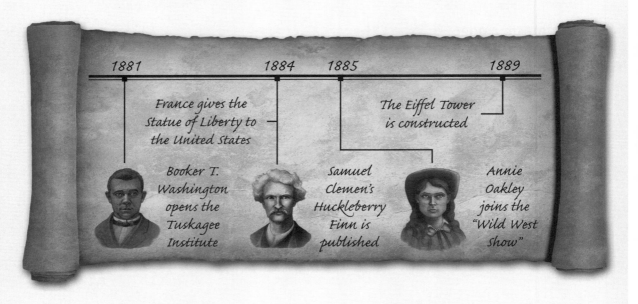

Activity

Tuskegee University in Alabama has a rich history and tradition. Learn more about it. What kind of degrees do they offer? How do you think they are carrying on the traditions started by Booker T. Washington? A famous group of airmen came from Tuskegee Institute during the Second World War. Who were they and what did they accomplish?

Wordscramble

Here is a list of scrambled words that relate to the profile you read about Booker T. Washington. Unscramble the letters and write the words correctly.

1. nBrongsiahotTokWe _____

2. mrrnSmstauAloge _____

3. ChvtWaoaniGesrgoegnrer _____

4. egrno _____

5. aitdnemeirotn _____

6. ensreeecpavr _____

7. oanpmtH _____

8. gittuIenketseseuT _____

9. aegcly _____

10. Isnilbtaae _____

Before and After

Read the event on the left side and the event on the right side. Then decide if the first event (on the left) happened **before** or **after** the second event (on the right). Choose the word in the middle column that is correct. You may circle the correct answer or draw a line from the words *before* or *after* to the matching event.

1	Booker T. Washington worked as a slave.	Before	After	Booker attended Hampton Institute in Virginia.
2	Booker started classes in his hometown.	Before	After	General Armstrong became his role model.
3	Booker became the head of Tuskegee Institute.	Before	After	Booker was invited to teach at Hampton Institute.
4	One hundred buildings were built at Tuskegee.	Before	After	Booker's first class was held at Tuskegee in a leaky, church building.
5	Booker founded the National Negro Business League.	Before	After	Booker's autobiography was published.

Booker T. Washington Word Search

```
R M A G W J L R S K J W O D V A O D A
X K G K M I N E G R O S F U V Y Q T B
K M N L I H B O E S J M Z G V L B B N
W Y X Z W B U D Q O M F F T Y A D Q
I S S A M U E L A R M S T R O N G Y N
Q P E R S E V E R A N C E J Z G U O B
S B O O K E R T W A S H I N G T O N X
K U F K I I Y O B M P G A Z H S L A X
M T T M A F F D U I W C Y J O C K D D
T U S K E G E E I N S T I T U T E J B
W E S G Z C E M O H L M I P Y X S Z B
H A M P T O N E L E G A C Y R T P R B
P G F J D E T E R M I N A T I O N Y D
V X I N S A T I A B L E Z U W H Z O P
B D Q O M G E O R G E W C A R V E R L
```

Word Bank

Booker T. Washington
determination
George Washington Carver
Hampton
legacy

negro
perseverance
Samuel Armstrong
Tuskegee Institute
Twentieth Maine

Booker T. Washington Crossword

Across

3. steady belief and determination over time, in spite of obstacles
5. school first led by Booker T. Washington
7. African American teacher and leader
9. an earlier term describing African Americans, or blacks
10. renowned teacher of agriculture at Tuskegee Institute

Down

1. not easily satisfied
2. something handed down from one generation to the next
4. Union General and principal of Hampton
6. having a firm purpose
8. school attended by Booker in Virginia

Samuel Clemens

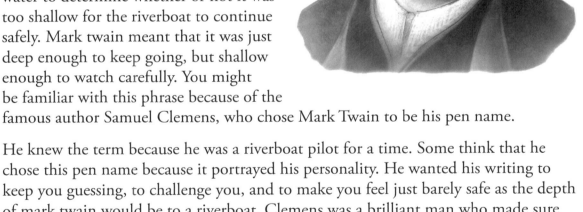

In the 1800s, a popular mode of transportation along the Mississippi river was a riverboat. The pilots of these boats were a little like a pilot of an airplane is today. They made a good living and were widely respected. Also like airplane pilots, they had a challenging job with many things to learn and remember. Mark twain is an old riverboat term that you might recognize. It measures the depth of two fathoms, or twelve feet. Someone would lower a marked pole into the water to determine whether or not it was too shallow for the riverboat to continue safely. Mark twain meant that it was just deep enough to keep going, but shallow enough to watch carefully. You might be familiar with this phrase because of the famous author Samuel Clemens, who chose Mark Twain to be his pen name.

He knew the term because he was a riverboat pilot for a time. Some think that he chose this pen name because it portrayed his personality. He wanted his writing to keep you guessing, to challenge you, and to make you feel just barely safe as the depth of mark twain would be to a riverboat. Clemens was a brilliant man who made sure that you had to work to find the deeper meaning in his words, and maybe go on an unexpected adventure along the way.

> *"Twenty years from now, you will be more disappointed by the things that you didn't do than by the ones you did do. So throw off the bowlines. Sail away from the safe harbor. Catch the trade winds in your sails. Explore. Dream. Discover."*

> -Mark Twain

His most famous work, *The Adventures of Huckleberry Finn*, is considered by many to be the first great American novel. In it, he gives us an example of real life in a small town, like the area he grew up in near Hannibal, Missouri. He used local dialect such as "ain't" to make his characters more lifelike. Before Mark Twain came along there weren't any famous stories about American culture. He believed in doing things his own way, and didn't apologize for it, which is often how people change history. They decide to go against the grain, to put their passions above their concern for public acceptance. In the 1800s, Europe's great authors such as Charles Dickens, Leo Tolstoy, Victor Hugo, and Jane Austin were the models when it came to writing. For most people, all they wanted to do was measure up to these unmatchable authors. Mark Twain decided to create his own model.

The *Adventures of Huckleberry Finn* (which is the sequel to *The Adventures of Tom Sawyer*) is a tale filled with colorful characters, comedy, exciting adventures, and great depth. Along with Huck, you take a journey of self-examination and growth. Another main character in the story is a runaway slave named Jim. The book paints a very sympathetic view of the difficulty in being a slave. This came during a time when people severely struggled with racism.

Not only did everyday readers appreciate his work, other authors recognized the quality of writing, depth, and originality found there as well. Another well-known American author said this of *The Adventures of Huckleberry Finn*:

> *"All modern American literature comes from one book by Mark Twain called 'Huckleberry Finn.' All American writing comes from that. There was nothing before. There has been nothing as good since."*

> -Ernest Hemingway

Like many other great artists, Samuel Clemens' life was sometimes controversial. But he used his many works to ask questions he thought were important. He challenged people to look at life realistically and to see the humor in their own circumstances.

"I came in with Halley's Comet in 1835. It is coming again next year (1910), and I expect to go out with it. It will be the greatest disappointment of my life if I don't go out with Halley's Comet. The Almighty has said, no doubt: 'Now here are these two unaccountable freaks; they came in together, they must go out together.'"

-Mark Twain

Just as he predicted, Mark Twain did go out with Halley's Comet. He lived a full life, with successes, failures, love, and laughter, and he certainly left his imprint on the world. Some of his other noteworthy works are *The Adventures of Tom Sawyer, A Connecticut Yankee in King Arthur's Court, The Prince and the Pauper,* and too many short stories to mention. He made a place for American authors on the world's stage.

Timeline Review

Put things in perspective. Place Samuel Clemens' figure on the timeline in the year 1884, which was when *Huckleberry Finn* was published. Look at the other events before, during, and after this year.

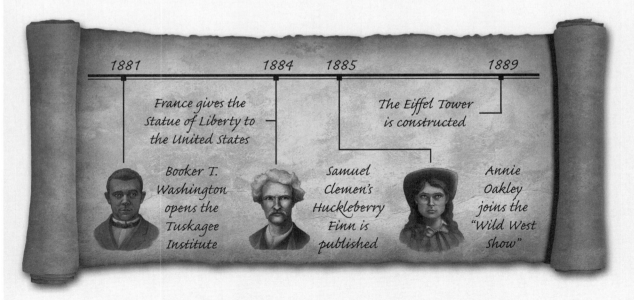

1881 — Booker T. Washington opens the Tuskagee Institute

1884 — France gives the Statue of Liberty to the United States

1885 — Samuel Clemen's Huckleberry Finn is published

— The Eiffel Tower is constructed

1889 — Annie Oakley joins the "Wild West show"

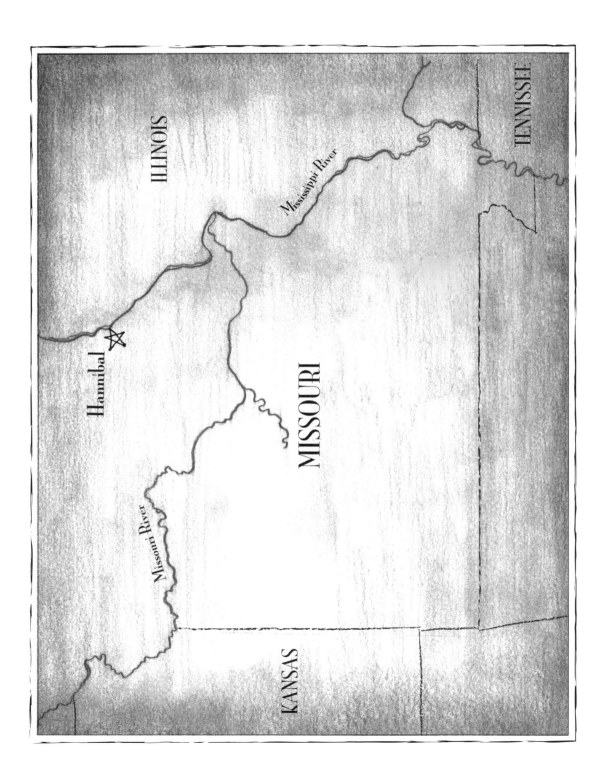

Discussion

Mark Twain used his life experiences as a starting point for his stories. Since he grew up near a river, he wrote about the people and places connected to river life. The struggles he observed during the Civil War were also a part of his writing. Good writing often comes from real life experience. Talk with your teacher or parent about experiences you have had that you think would make a good story.

Activity

Some of Mark Twain's works are more suited to children. Several of these books have abridged, or easier to read, versions as well as videos. Talk with your parents about these stories and with their permission, read or watch a video presentation of one of his stories. Afterwards, tell what you think about the way he presented his characters. Did they seem realistic to you? What main ideas or lessons did you learn from the story?

Wordscramble

Here is a list of scrambled words that relate to the profile you read about Samuel Clemens. Unscramble the letters and write the words correctly.

1. MaiarTnwk _____

2. eaelsmeulmCnS _____

3. biltinrla _____

4. oelnv _____

5. transliovorce _____

6. sioriMsu _____

7. lvpirioaobtetr _____

8. ebFrrHulekinycn _____

9. laytCeoelHms _____

10. HnieEmstrygeawn _____

Using Context

Read the sentence and then look at the word in *italics*. Tell what you think that word means. Then look it up in a dictionary to confirm, or make sure of, the meaning. Tell someone about each word that you got correct. Remember, you will get better at understanding word meanings as you practice using context, or the words around a word.

1. Clemens was a *brilliant* man who made sure that you had to work to find the deeper meaning in his words, and maybe go on an unexpected adventure along the way. (paragraph 2)

   I think *brilliant* means: _____

   Dictionary definition: _____

   My meaning was: (Circle one)   correct   had correct parts   not close

2. His most famous work, *The Adventures of Huckleberry Finn*, is considered by many to be the first great American *novel*. (paragraph 4)

   I think *novel* means: _____

   Dictionary definition: _____

   My meaning was: (Circle one)   correct   had correct parts   not close

3. Like many other great artists, his life was sometimes *controversial*, but he used his many works to ask questions he thought were important. (paragraph 8)

   I think *controversial* means: _____

   Dictionary definition: _____

   My meaning was: (Circle one)   correct   had correct parts   not close

Samuel Clemens Word Search

```
B  W  X  S  G  A  T  C  E  G  M  D  R  O  O  T  N  R  L
R  R  D  A  I  V  Y  V  Q  K  U  P  S  D  N  W  D  I  Q
I  I  N  M  V  M  I  S  S  O  U  R  I  R  K  A  G  V  R
L  L  H  U  C  K  L  E  B  E  R  R  Y  F  I  N  N  E  X
L  V  S  E  A  J  Q  C  H  K  C  I  W  B  N  M  D  R  Y
I  X  J  L  A  T  D  F  U  U  U  M  J  K  W  L  B  V
A  L  A  C  T  E  E  M  C  M  A  A  O  P  V  I  O  P
N  D  M  L  C  O  N  T  R  O  V  E  R  S  I  A  L  A  Y
T  P  R  E  H  G  C  B  U  T  H  F  K  N  T  N  U  T  M
N  R  T  M  Q  Z  V  Q  F  H  X  F  T  D  H  S  V  P  C
E  R  N  E  S  T  H  E  M  I  N  G  W  A  Y  M  E  I  X
A  V  Z  N  D  I  R  D  I  A  J  X  A  U  Z  N  C  L  Y
W  I  L  S  I  Q  N  O  V  E  L  X  I  O  F  J  Q  O  M
K  H  Z  P  Y  Q  X  B  M  Z  G  Q  N  H  W  J  S  T  V
Z  H  A  L  L  E  Y  S  C  O  M  E  T  D  A  N  A  M  U
```

Word Bank

brilliant

controversial

Ernest Hemingway

Halley's Comet

Huckleberry Finn

Mark Twain

Missouri

novel

riverboat pilot

Samuel Clemens

Samuel Clemens Crossword

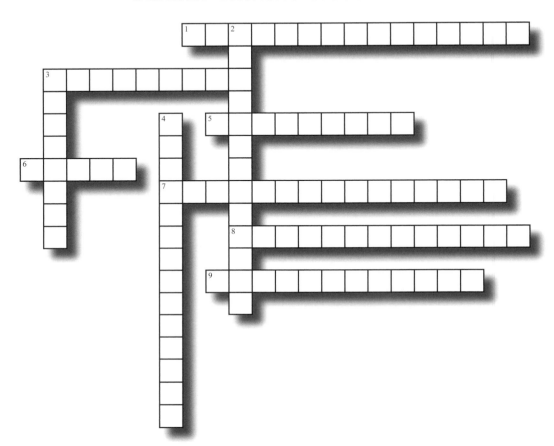

Across

1. one of Mark Twain's characters
3. pen name of Samuel Clemens
5. showing exceptional talent
6. a work of fiction, usually divided into chapters with complex plot and characters
7. famous American author
8. real name of author Mark Twain
9. a comet that passes Earth approximately every 76 years

Down

2. something that creates strong disagreement in public conversations
3. Mark Twain's home state
4. someone who directs, or steers a riverboat

Annie Oakley

Celebrity is "the state of being famous." There are many celebrities today that children and young adults look up to. Undoubtedly, some are movie stars, athletes, and musicians. What is it about celebrities that inspire such admiration? Is it curiosity? Is it the desire to imitate? Who is really worthy of this kind of admiration? Who would you want others to look up to?

During the late 1800s, Annie Oakley became one of the first American superstars. In addition to her great talent, Annie's genuine kindness and lovable personality thrust her into the hearts of America. Young girls all over the country looked up to this gracious and humble woman. Annie overcame a tragic childhood and became an inspiration to children everywhere. She is the picture of determination and integrity. Annie is worthy of remembrance because she gave young women and children a role model.

Annie was born in Darke County, Ohio. She was forced to grow up quickly when her father died after returning home from a visit into town. Unfortunately, a snowstorm developed while he was out, and he was unable to recover from the effects. Annie had six other brothers and sisters that her mother now had to take care of.

After the death of her husband, Annie's mother soon realized that she was unable to provide for so many children. She did the best she could for a few years, but when Annie was about ten years old, her mother decided it would be better for her to live at the local infirmary, or poor farm. This was a government run facility where children whose parents couldn't afford them anymore could be sent. Orphans and mentally and physically handicapped people also lived there. Not long after she arrived, Annie was lent to a farmer who claimed he would send her to school and take care of her. He promised she would be cared for like a member of the family, and all she had to do was help with chores around the farm. Annie soon found out that he did not intend to keep his promise. In her later years, she would only refer to them as "the wolves." They treated Annie like a slave or worse, forcing her to work constantly and most likely beating her. One day when she noticed they weren't home, Annie left. She started walking and never looked back.

Finally, in her teenage years, Annie was able to move back home with her family. Her mother had remarried, but times were still hard. Annie had taken her very first shots when she found her father's gun some years before, and now that she was home again hunting became her full-time job. She loved being outside and able to provide meals for her family, and she loved shooting. Her reputation as a hunter of game, or animals, soon spread throughout the small town. Some people might wonder how Annie Oakley became the best female shooter of her time. The answer is she taught herself. She started shooting out of necessity, but she kept shooting because she loved it.

Frank Butler, a handsome sharpshooter, had taken his act on the road with a traveling circus, when his life took a fateful turn. While traveling through the town of Cincinnati, Ohio, he entered a shooting contest with an unknown local. Whoever won would get a prize of $100. Since Frank needed the money at the time, he agreed. Little did he know that the unknown shooter was a young woman who didn't even look strong enough to hold a rifle, much less shoot it. To his surprise five-foot tall, slender Annie could shoot. She beat him in the contest, but instead of bitterness or anger at defeat by a woman, Frank was intrigued. He invited Annie to come see his act in Cincinnati, and the two soon fell deeply in love. They were married about a year later. Annie Oakley's husband became her biggest supporter. He always traveled with her, took care of her, and once he realized that her talent far exceeded his, he dropped his own act and became her manager. For a girl with such a distraught childhood, her later years were certainly happy ones.

After meeting Frank, Annie made another acquaintance that would change her life forever. His name was William F. Cody, better known as Buffalo Bill. Buffalo Bill started a Wild West Show that eventually became famous worldwide. He created a grand picture of the Wild West for his audiences—with cowboys, Indians, horses, buffalo, excitement, and entertainment. The addition of Annie Oakley's sharpshooting soon became a crowd favorite. Everyone looked forward to seeing the petite, mild mannered Annie step forward with her shotgun and stun the audience with her accuracy and skill. Annie learned many of her tricks from Frank, who assisted her with various props and stunts during the show. Although she was pressured to take advantage of the fact that she was a woman in the show, Annie never compromised her beliefs. She made all of her own costumes, and they were always modest from the beginning of her career to the end.

Annie Oakley has been called one of the greatest women shooters of all time. Even greater than her shooting though, was her character. Her recognition represented a change, and many women gained courage from that. Throughout her lifetime Annie taught over 1,000 women how to shoot a gun. Due to the hardships she suffered as a child, Annie always paid special attention to children, giving to many charities that supported them. During World War I, Annie and Frank offered their time and talent to train soldiers in the art of shooting. Frank always shared in her conviction and desire to do what she could for the world around her. From the day they married, Annie and her husband were practically inseparable. When she died at the age of sixty-six, Frank passed away only eighteen days later.

Annie Oakley was truly a star in her day. She met royalty and traveled the world, yet always remained a person worthy of the admiration she was given. Annie caught the attention of the world and gained the respect of a nation. She taught America what a true celebrity could look like.

Discussion

People with different jobs are celebrities today, such as actors, musicians, and athletes. The skill they display in these areas and the high amounts of money they are paid seem to make others, especially young people, want to be like them. Annie was very concerned about her reputation, or the way people thought of her. Talk with your teacher or parent about what you think makes someone a good role model, or example for others to follow. Think of at least one example of a good role model and one example of someone you think is not a good role model. Talk about the ways they are different.

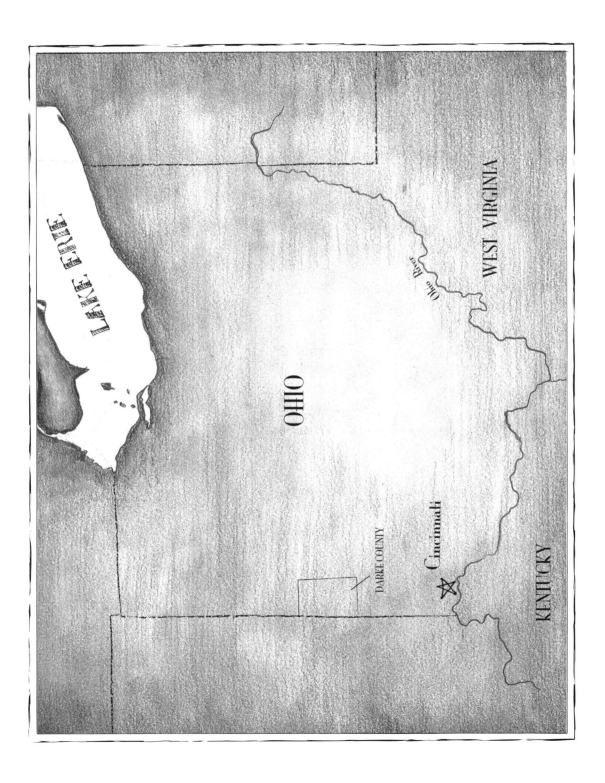

Timeline Review

Put things in perspective. Place Annie Oakley's figure on the timeline in the year 1885, which was when she joined the "Wild West Show." Look at the other events before, during, and after this year.

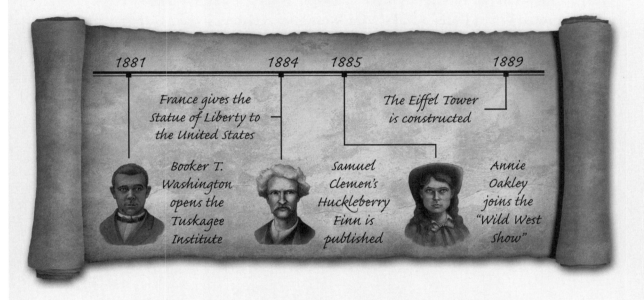

1881 — France gives the Statue of Liberty to the United States

1884 — Booker T. Washington opens the Tuskagee Institute

1885 — Samuel Clemen's Huckleberry Finn is published

The Eiffel Tower is constructed

1889 — Annie Oakley joins the "Wild West Show"

Activity

For many people, America's westward growth and the taming of the rough conditions encountered there made the old West a place of great stories about bravery and daring. Those who did not live there read of characters from the West in books and magazines. Many of the stories made the West and the figures in it very brave and adventurous. When Buffalo Bill's Wild West Show started, it gave everyday people a chance to see a part of the old West. Learn more about Buffalo Bill's Wild West Show. Now think about rodeos. Many of the events in rodeos came from skills needed to work with horses and cattle. Learn about rodeos. How do you think rodeos and Buffalo Bill's show are the same? How are they different?

Wordscramble

Here is a list of scrambled words that relate to the profile you read about Annie Oakley. Unscramble the letters and write the words correctly.

1. AilenkaneOy _____
2. ruBtkFearln _____
3. uBalfoBlfil _____
4. osahrhprsoet _____
5. WhisletSoWwd _____

6. anukrtDyeCo _____
7. ryicbetle _____
8. moleledor _____
9. nniopcmmrgosiu _____
10. mniainetteord _____

Before and After

Read the event on the left side and the event on the right side. Then decide if the first event (on the left) happened **before** or **after** the second event (on the right). Choose the word in the middle column that is correct. You may circle the correct answer or draw a line from the words *before* or *after* to the matching event.

1	Annie's father died.	Before	After	Annie became a famous sharpshooter.
2	Annie started shooting game for food and to sell.	Before	After	Annie walked away from the home where she was sent to work.
3	Annie met Buffalo Bill Cody.	Before	After	Annie met her future husband, Frank Butler.
4	Annie became a famous sharpshooter.	Before	After	Annie and Frank helped train soldiers to shoot.
5	Annie traveled the world and met kings and queens.	Before	After	Annie started making her own costumes.

Annie Oakley Word Search

```
U A M J I M Z C H V A T I A N U W V B
X I F X T S I S Z P C A B S N N H X M
R Q A R B Z Q H B V E G U L D C U V R
N U N Z X D M A F Y L Y F J Y O S U T
F E N S J Z A R E X E U F C J M B C M
D S I M W X W P K P B P A C U P L Q T
B Q E E I J E S T M R O L S J R M K U
S G O G D K S H U S I Y O F S O F K A
Y D A R K E C O U N T Y B G R M K Y D
C H K F C Y H O I J Y F I K D I G E O
W I L D W E S T S H O W L B F S I V E
V H E O R O L E M O D E L C F I U O R
M U Y D E T E R M I N A T I O N I K V
U C B T P R Y T B A X S Z W T G M V X
Y O X H K F R A N K B U T L E R P K Y
```

Word Bank

Annie Oakley
Frank Butler
Buffalo Bill
sharpshooter
Wild West Show

Darke County
celebrity
role model
uncompromising
determination

Annie Oakley Crossword

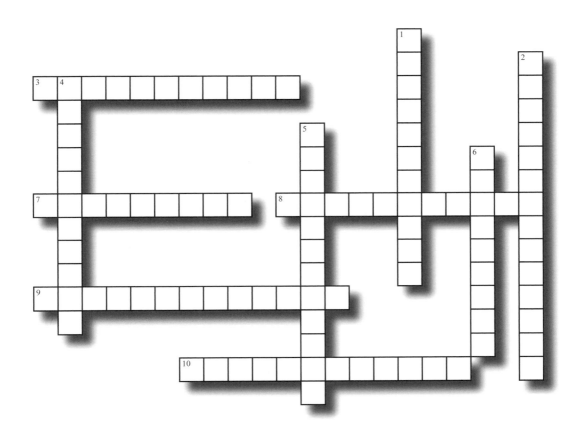

Across

3. Annie Oakley's birthplace
7. someone to be looked up to, an example
8. Annie Oakley's husband
9. showing a firm will or purpose
10. a show about the West started by Buffalo Bill Cody

Down

1. the nickname of William Cody
2. showing no willingness to back down or give up
4. famous woman skilled at shooting
5. someone very good at hitting a target by firing a gun
6. a person who is famous during his or her lifetime

John Philip Sousa

Who are the most memorable people throughout history? Often politicians and great leaders change the world, though not everyone changes the world through politics or leadership. Sometimes change can come in a more subtle form. Many kinds of talent can bring about change, and each one has its place.

Patrick Henry made a speech that inspired the delegates representing our nation to stand up and vote for independence. Joshua Chamberlain played one part in a battle that possibly changed the outcome of the Civil War. Samuel Clemens, or Mark Twain, forever changed what people thought about American writing. Everyone has a part to play, and each is different. For John Philip Sousa's part, change came through music.

Sousa was surrounded by music from the time he was born. His father played the trombone in the United States Marine Band, also known as the President's Own.

Sousa grew up in Washington, D.C. during a time when our country was at war with itself. Sousa's father was among those in the Marine Band who played during Abraham Lincoln's inauguration, as well as his funeral. Since he was in Washington at a time of war, Sousa heard many military bands while growing up. Later known as the March King, undoubtedly his upbringing affected the music for which he would be famous.

John started playing the violin when he was only six years old, and he could play several other instruments by the time he was ten. At the young age of thirteen, Sousa's father signed him up to be part of the Marine Corps Band. For seven years John

Philip Sousa learned from his father and the other musicians of the Marine Band. After that time, John was ready for an adventure. He played violin professionally, worked as a composer, conducted orchestras, and traveled to various towns to perform. John met his wife, Jane Bellis, who was a singer, during his days of traveling. The couple enjoyed many happy years of marriage and had three children.

John Philip Sousa gained much respect as a musician and composer during this time. The Marine Band took notice of Sousa's growing reputation, and in the year 1880 they invited him to come back. This time though, he returned as their leader. John had very definite ideas about how the band should be run. As soon as he became its leader, he filtered out some of the musicians that he thought weren't committed, and added some new ones who would bring talent and strength to the band. Sousa led the Marine Band from its previously average state to a place of worldwide recognition, and brought great respect to this representation of American music. It was he who started a tradition of greatness that is still in practice today. Sousa was leader of the U.S. Marine Band for twelve years, and he served five different presidents during that time. Not only was he a musician, conductor, and composer, but Sousa was also a writer who published several books and articles. He was also an excellent trap shooter.

John resigned from the Marine Band in 1892. After that he started putting together a group of very elite musicians that would soon be known worldwide as the Sousa Band. John enjoyed many tours with the Sousa Band. Some went all across the country. They were so famous that when they arrived in a town, school was canceled and people took the day off from work so that everyone could attend the concert. The Sousa Band also did several tours in Europe and other places around the world.

It was on his way home from a vacation with his wife that Sousa said he began to hear music playing in his head. From those notes came a masterpiece that would be forever linked with his name and with America. When Sousa arrived home after that trip, he quickly wrote down all the notes just as he had heard them. And thus, his most famous march, "The Stars and Stripes Forever," came into being. Sousa believed that he was divinely inspired that day. Oftentimes when people hear it, they become so moved that they stand to their feet in honor of its magnitude. Sousa's patriotism was undeniable, and during his marches people could feel it coming through the notes. While Ronald Reagan was President it was decided that "The Stars and Stripes

Forever" would be the official march of the United States. Sousa even wrote lyrics to go along with the music. This is the first verse:

> *"Let martial note in triumph float*
> *And liberty extend its mighty hand*
> *A flag appears 'mid thunderous cheers,*
> *The banner of the Western land.*
> *The emblem of the brave and true*
> *Its folds protect no tyrant crew;*
> *The red and white and starry blue*
> *Is freedom's shield and hope."*

John Philip Sousa was one of the first great American composers. If you attend a Fourth of July celebration or another patriotic event, you will most likely hear one of his famous compositions. John's music will always make his country proud wherever it is played. Fittingly, the very last piece of music Sousa ever conducted was the one that he would be most remembered for, "The Stars and Stripes Forever."

Discussion

One of the most important qualities of music is that it can inspire, or encourage, enthusiasm in us. Certain types of music are played in settings where many people have gathered, such as concerts or parades to honor our country. Music written to express pride in one's country can be especially inspiring. Marches are one type of music often played in this setting. Can you think of a song, such as the National Anthem, that inspires feelings of pride for your country? Listen to "The Stars and Stripes Forever." Read the full lyrics that John Philip Sousa wrote for the march, and then sing them along with the music. Do you feel like this song is a good representation of American patriotism?

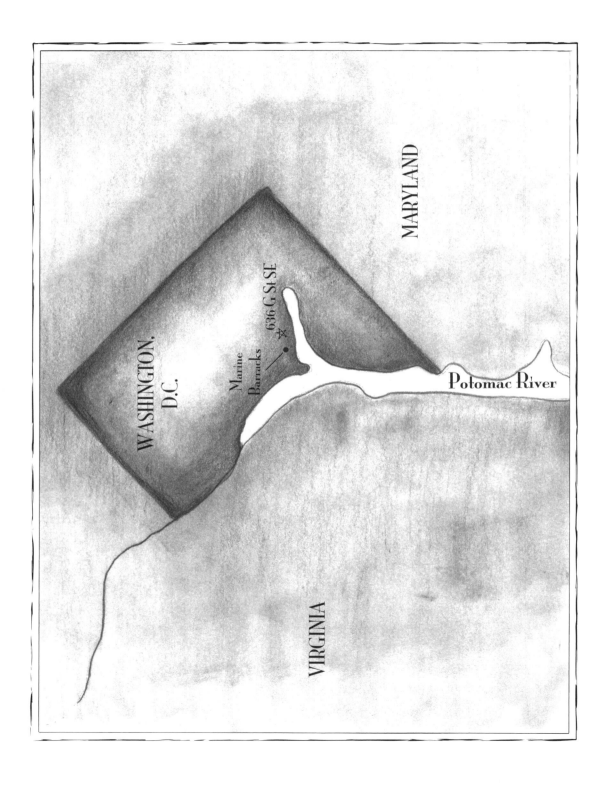

Timeline Review

Put things in perspective. Place John Philip Sousa's figure on the timeline in the year 1896, which was when he composed "The Stars and Stripes Forever." Look at the other events before, during, and after this year.

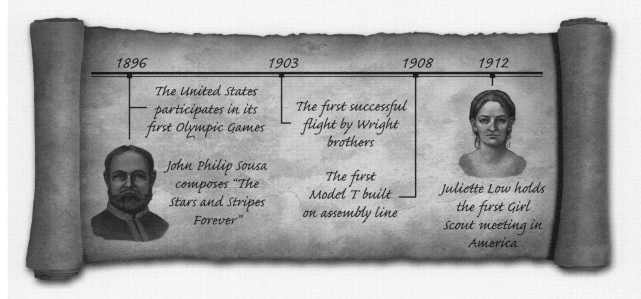

Activity

As a composer, or writer of music, John Philip Sousa was very knowledgeable about instruments and the sounds they make—especially brass instruments used in the music he wrote. To create a particular sound, some composers invented special instruments. Learn more about the sousaphone, named after its inventor, John Philip Sousa. What does it look like and how does it sound? How does it particularly fit the type of music he wrote and enjoyed playing? Tell your teacher or parent why you think Sousa created this instrument.

Wordscramble

Here is a list of scrambled words that relate to the profile you read about John Philip Sousa. Unscramble the letters and write the words correctly.

1. aslhJiopiohPnSu _____

2. elisaenlJB _____

3. tnWnDoasCigh _____

4. nsdauaBoS _____

5. BrMdaenani _____

6. giKnhrMca _____

7. nmciasiu _____

8. cootndruc _____

9. cosperom _____

10. ielte _____

Using Context

Read the sentence and then look at the word in *italics*. Tell what you think that word means. Then look it up in a dictionary to confirm, or make sure of, the meaning. Tell someone about each word that you got correct. Remember, you will get better at understanding word meanings as you practice using context, or the words around a word.

1. He played violin professionally, became a *composer*, conducted orchestras, and traveled to various towns to perform. (paragraph 4)

   I think *composer* means: _____

   Dictionary definition: _____

   My meaning was: (Circle one)   correct   had correct parts   not close

2. Not only was he a musician, *conductor*, and composer, but Sousa was also a writer who published several books and articles. (paragraph 5)

   I think *conductor* means: _____

   Dictionary definition: _____

   My meaning was: (Circle one)   correct   had correct parts   not close

3. After that he started putting together a group of very *elite* musicians that would soon be known worldwide as the Sousa Band. (paragraph 6)

   I think *elite* means: _____

   Dictionary definition: _____

   My meaning was: (Circle one)   correct   had correct parts   not close

John Philip Sousa Word Search

```
U A M J I M Z C H V A T I A N F W V B
X I F X J A N E B E L L I S N L H X M
R Q P R B Z Q L B V E G K L D W U V R
N U L Z X D M I F Y G S C Y Z S U T
F E F S J Z A T E X O U Z O J M B C M
D S G M W X W E K P U M V N U R L Q T
B Q C E I J E W T M O U A D J Y M K U
S J O H N P H I L I P S O U S A F K A
Y J M A R C H K I N G I M C R I K Y D
C H P F C Y H N I J G C Y T D D G E O
E O O E Y C L M Y G M I P O F Q I V E
V H S O U S A B A N D A Z R F H U O R
M U E E B H W A S H I N G T O N D C V
M A R I N E B A N D X S Z W T W M V X
Y O X H K P X S W L X L R V M Z P K Y
```

Word Bank

composer
conductor
elite
Jane Bellis
John Philip Sousa

March King
Marine Band
musician
Sousa Band
Washington, D.C.

John Philip Sousa Crossword

Across

4. the city in which Sousa grew up
6. someone who conducts a group of musicians
7. a small group with special standing
8. the band that Sousa started after he resigned from the Marine Band
9. someone who plays music, often professionally
10. John Philip Sousa's wife

Down

1. the band representing the U. S. Marines which Sousa led for 12 years
2. the nickname given to Sousa because of his famous music
3. famous American composer
5. a person who writes music

Juliette Low

"Girl Scouting builds girls of courage, confidence, and character, who make the world a better place."

The Girl Scout Mission

Juliette Low had a dream. She wanted to create an organization for girls that would bring them together, prepare them for life, and equip them for the future. The fulfillment of the dream came in the year 1912. Juliette, also known as Daisy, held the first Girl Scout meeting in her hometown of Savannah, Georgia. Eighteen young girls came to that first meeting. From there, the Girl Scout movement began to grow rapidly throughout the nation. Today, there are over three million members.

Juliette Low was born into a very prominent family in the high society of Savannah. Throughout her years she was able to travel overseas, attend socialite parties, and generally take pleasure in living a very comfortable life. Most women in her position would have been content to just enjoy the luxuries of that life. Juliette, however, was not. She wanted to do something lasting with her time and her prosperity. It wasn't until 1911 when she met Sir Robert Baden-Powell, founder of the Boy Scouts, that she knew how she wanted to leave a worthwhile inheritance for future generations. At the age of 51 Juliette Low had found her calling.

Low devoted her time and her money to get the Girl Scouts started. Her fortune was the main source of financial support in the early years of the organization. Juliette had enjoyed many luxuries when she was a young girl. She understood that money enabled her to do things that most young girls never got to experience. Her goal was for the Girl Scouts to provide a vehicle for girls of any situation to gain positive experiences. Juliette saw firsthand how the socialite world could exclude the less fortunate or handicapped, and she didn't want that to happen in her organization.

Due to chronic ear infections, Juliette lost much of her hearing in one ear. Then, on her wedding day, Low unfortunately got a piece of celebratory "wedding rice" lodged in her good ear. When doctors attempted to remove it, her eardrum was punctured, and she became completely deaf in that ear. Low's intention was that the Girl Scouts would be "something for all the girls," not just the wealthy, not just for one race or one culture, but for all. During that day and age, physically disabled girls were not welcome to participate in many group activities. That was not to be so with the Girl Scouts. Low never let her almost total deafness keep her from embracing life. She was determined not to let physical disabilities hold other girls back either.

During the First and Second World Wars, the Girl Scouts took it upon themselves to do what they could for the war effort. They came up with many creative ways to help the soldiers overseas and the families back at home. During the Great Depression, the Girl Scouts raised funds and gathered food and clothing for the most needy. They teamed up with First Ladies Nancy Reagan for the "Just Say No to Drugs" campaign as well as Barbara Bush during the "Right to Read" project, fighting illiteracy.

Girl Scouts everywhere have become responsible citizens, helped during times of great need, cared for the environment, aided in their communities, built friendships, and had a lot of fun. For about 100 years, the Girl Scouts organization has educated and empowered young women of all backgrounds. All of this became possible because of the determination and vision of one Juliette Low. Her home in Savannah, Georgia, was designated a National Historic Landmark, and many devoted Girl Scouts have made the trip to visit the site of their founder's home. It is with gratitude to Juliette "Daisy" Low, called "the Best Scout," that we honor the Girl Scouts of the world and all they have done.

Discussion

Though Juliette Low grew up in a wealthy family, she learned about others living around her who were less fortunate. Although money certainly isn't the basis for happiness, it is helpful when trying to accomplish certain goals. The Girl Scouts fulfilled Juliette Low's desire to help others. However, there are many ways to be of help to your community. Talk with your parents about the ways you would like to help others. Can you observe them as they lend a hand in your community? Remember that small contributions are just as important as large ones.

Timeline Review

Put things in perspective. Place Juliette Low's figure on the timeline in the year 1912, which was when she held the first Girl Scout meeting. Look at the other events before, during and after this year.

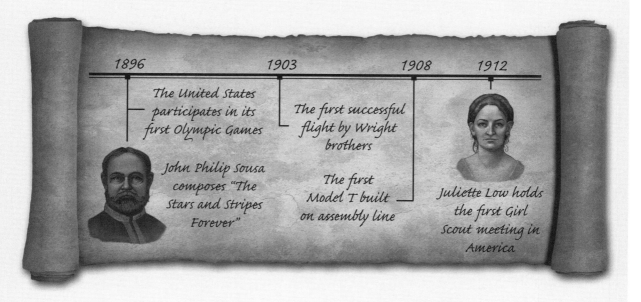

1896 — The United States participates in its first Olympic Games

John Philip Sousa composes "The Stars and Stripes Forever"

1903 — The first successful flight by Wright brothers

The first Model T built on assembly line

1908

1912 — Juliette Low holds the first Girl Scout meeting in America

Activity

Learn more about the Girl Scouts. Well known for many things, including learning about a variety of topics and earning badges to show their knowledge, holding nation-wide cookie sales to raise funds, and many outdoor activities, read about the Girl Scouts or the Boy Scouts if you prefer. Make a list of at least five things that you did not know about scouting. If you are a scout, think about what you feel is the best thing about that organization. If you aren't a scout, ask someone who is what he or she thinks is the best thing.

Wordscramble

Here is a list of scrambled words that relate to the profile you read about Juliette Low. Unscramble the letters and write the words correctly.

1. ueoJtewitlL _____

2. ebdewRoltrlePBnao _____

3. orSiGsctlu _____

4. eBcutstoS _____

5. naavanSh _____

6. ueoagrc _____

7. ndocniefec _____

8. rcrcaaeth _____

9. sceiaitlo _____

10. iDsay _____

Before and After

Read the event on the left side and the event on the right side. Then decide if the first event (on the left) happened **before** or **after** the second event (on the right). Choose the word in the middle column that is correct. You may circle the correct answer or draw a line from the words *before* or *after* to the matching event.

1	Juliette Low was a young socialite in Savannah.	Before	After	The first meeting of the Girl Scouts was held.
2	Juliette decided how she wanted to spend her time and money.	Before	After	Juliette met Sir Robert Baden-Powell.
3	Juliette had lost most of her hearing.	Before	After	She decided to include girls with physical handicaps in the Girl Scouts.
4	Girl Scouts participated in the programs of First Ladies Nancy Reagan and Barbara Bush.	Before	After	Girls Scouts helped raise funds during the Great Depression.
5	Juliette Low's home in Savannah was named a National Historic Landmark.	Before	After	Many American girls began participating in Girl Scouts.

Juliette Low Word Search

```
S  A  R  V  E  G  I  R  L  S  C  O  U  T  S  K  Z  C  J
K  K  J  V  F  G  E  Z  P  U  G  W  W  T  U  U  H  W  T
K  A  I  J  C  O  U  R  A  G  E  A  R  K  W  E  H  E  K
U  H  Q  S  H  G  N  G  N  J  Q  Y  N  W  N  J  V  X  J
X  S  D  Z  A  V  L  S  P  V  I  U  C  T  F  U  W  X  V
R  O  B  E  R  T  B  A  D  E  N  P  O  W  E  L  L  D  Q
B  C  O  T  A  C  O  V  A  F  E  J  N  Q  C  I  B  L  N
V  I  M  K  C  N  S  A  I  E  G  U  F  A  K  E  M  D  V
K  A  D  D  T  S  K  N  S  S  U  I  I  Y  E  T  K  A  H
Z  L  V  O  E  P  K  N  Y  J  A  M  D  W  Z  T  P  B  E
K  I  V  C  R  Y  N  A  Q  R  U  J  E  G  E  E  D  O  C
T  T  J  S  Z  X  Y  H  A  X  R  W  N  S  N  L  V  C  C
Q  E  S  L  U  F  S  S  D  X  Y  F  C  K  B  O  A  K  H
A  P  O  A  C  S  S  K  S  R  M  I  E  L  H  W  S  M  M
Y  B  F  S  I  L  M  Y  Z  B  E  S  T  S  C  O  U  T  N
```

Word Bank

Best Scout

character

confidence

courage

Daisy

Girl Scouts

Juliette Low

Robert Baden-Powell

Savannah

socialite

Juliette Low Crossword

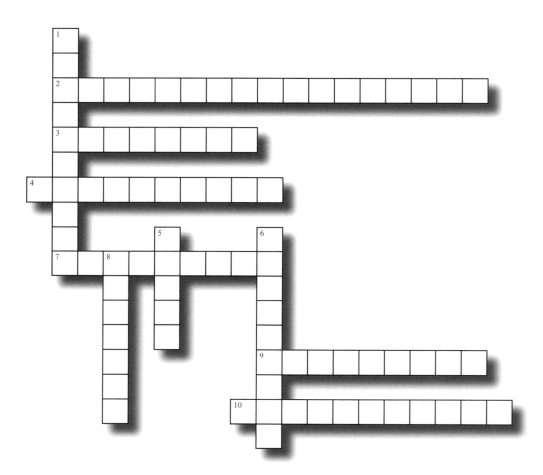

Across

2. founder of the Boy Scouts

3. a city on the coast of Georgia

4. the belief that you will be successful

7. a person well known in fashionable society

9. the qualities that show a person's thoughts and intentions

10. founder of the Girl Scouts

Down

1. the organization started by Low in 1912

5. Juliette Low's nickname

6. a title given to Juliette Low

8. the ability to face and overcome fear or danger

Will Rogers

Will Rogers is included in this compilation of outstanding Americans because he gave this country something that it was in desperate need of during his time— hope and humor. He gave a lighthearted interpretation of world news, politics, current events, and anything else in which the American public might be interested. Even through the country's hardest times, Will was there to cheer up a somber crowd or a worried reader. He is famous for sayings such as:

"I never met a man I didn't like."

"Even if you're on the right track, you'll get run over if you just sit there."

"I am just an old country boy in a big town trying to get along."

"Live your life so that whenever you lose, you are ahead."

Will was born on a ranch in Indian Territory, now known as Oklahoma. His parents were part Cherokee Indian, a fact of which he was always proud. He stated, "My ancestors didn't come on the Mayflower, but they met the boat." Will grew up herding cattle on his parent's ranch and living the life of a cowboy. As he got older however, Will began to get restless. Looking for adventure he traveled the world with a Wild West Show as a trick roper, joined a circus, and later became a performer in vaudeville. In 1916, Will joined the famous Broadway productions called the Zeigfeld Follies. New York City was the destination for stage performers in America during the early 1900's, and Will Rogers spent many years visiting and living there. He also starred in movies, became a columnist for the newspaper, and began a series of radio broadcasts. During this time he had many professional successes, but he considered his greatest triumph to be a personal one. Will Rogers married Betty Blake in 1908, and in his typical western fashion, here's how he described it:

"When I roped her, that was the star performance of my life."

Even though Will appeared on stage and screen, he gained a reputation as the voice of the common man. About forty million people looked forward to regularly reading his newspaper column. Not only did they enjoy his wit, but he also reported world news in a simple and easy to understand way. Will believed that everyone should stay in touch with current events and was famous for his opinions on them, or as he put it:

"I only know what I read in the newspaper."

During the year 1929, the United States began falling into the worst economic times it has ever seen. October 29, 1929, or "Black Tuesday," will forever mark the horrific day that the stock market crashed. After that, the American and world economies followed a steady decline that would last for about ten years. Twenty-five percent of Americans lost their jobs and many were without the basics of life, such as a home or food. The average American was living in a stress-filled world, with little to look forward to. So what was it then that could lift the hearts of these desperate people?

Although Will Rogers couldn't help everyone, he tried. He couldn't wave a magic wand and make all the world's problems go away, but he could make people forget about their troubles, at least for a little while. Have you ever heard the term "laughter is the best medicine?" It's true, especially when hope of recovery has dwindled and worry seems to be all that is left. So Will Rogers made people laugh—at themselves, at politics, and at the everyday struggles of life. He was a popular humorist from the 1920s until the year of his death in 1935. America needed him during the Great Depression of the 1930s, and Will was there for them as long as he could be.

Will died in a plane crash on his way to Point Barrow, Alaska. His friend, a famous pilot by the name of Wiley Post, was flying the plane. The best way to describe what Will Rogers' affable personality and humor meant to Americans is to look at their reaction to losing him. John McCormack, a world famous tenor and recording artist, said this of Will's tragic death:

"A smile has disappeared from the lips of America."

Will Rogers once said, "You must judge a man's greatness by how much he will be missed." By his own measurement, we can conclude that Will Rogers was a great man. Many have compared the outpouring of mourning for him to that of a beloved president. Damon Runyon, a newspaperman in New York, wrote that Will Rogers "reflected in many ways the heartbeat of America." The outpouring may have come about because every person who saw his movies, listened to him on the radio, or read his column in the newspaper everyday felt as though they knew him. They felt as though they'd lost a friend who not only made them laugh, but cared for them as well.

Discussion

The saying, "laughter is the best medicine" is very famous. Talk with your teacher or parent about what you think it means. How do you think laughter could do the same job as medicine? Have you ever experienced a time when your circumstances seemed sad or difficult, and laughter with family or while watching a video helped you to feel better? If you think laughter is helpful, be on the lookout for ways to encourage others who may be discouraged or sad by making them laugh. Prepare jokes, stories, or a clever video to share with others.

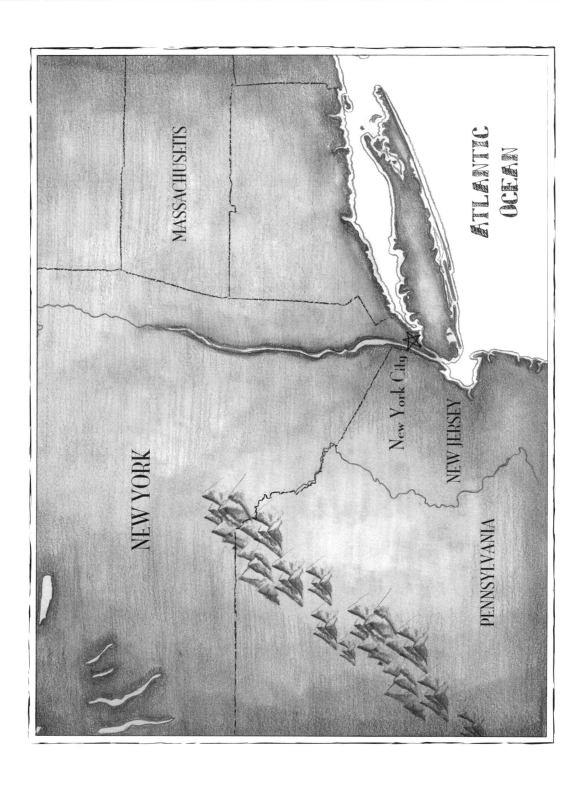

Timeline Review

Put things in perspective. Place Will Rogerst's figure on the timeline in the year 1922, which was when he began his career as a columnist. Look at the other events before, during, and after this year.

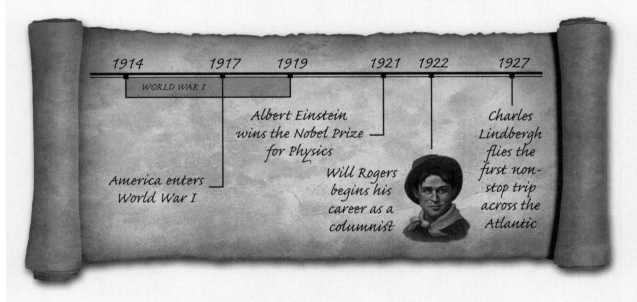

Activity

Successfully using a rope was a skill needed by every cowboy. Since Will Rogers grew up as a cowboy, he learned many of these types of skills. Later, he incorporated rope tricks into his show and they became a famous part of his act. Learn more about rope tricks. With your parents' permission, you may want to try to learn a few.

(The Will Rogers Rope Tricks set is available from Vision Forum, www.visionforum.com.)

Wordscramble

Here is a list of scrambled words that relate to the profile you read about Will Rogers. Unscramble the letters and write the words correctly.

1. lsloReWigr _____

2. lttkBeyBea _____

3. rpore _____

4. mituhsor _____

5. oeeChrek _____

6. ahmOoalk _____

7. sTelcaykaudB _____

8. ipertseDroGesna _____

9. ldeveaivlu _____

10. mlcniuost _____

Using Context

Read the sentence and then look at the word in *italics*. Tell what you think that word means. Then look it up in a dictionary to confirm, or make sure of, the meaning. Tell someone about each word that you got correct. Remember, you will get better at understanding word meanings as you practice using context, or the words around a word.

1. Looking for adventure he traveled the world with a Wild West Show as a trick roper, joined a circus, and later became a performer in *vaudeville*. (paragraph 3)

   I think *vaudeville* means: _____

   Dictionary definition: _____

   My meaning was: (Circle one)   correct   had correct parts   not close

2. He starred in movies, became a *columnist* for the newspaper, and began a series of radio broadcasts. (paragraph 3)

   I think *columnist* means: _____

   Dictionary definition: _____

   My meaning was: (Circle one)   correct   had correct parts   not close

3. He was a popular *humorist* from the 1920s until the year of his death in 1935. (paragraph 6)

   I think *humorist* means: _____

   Dictionary definition: _____

   My meaning was: (Circle one)   correct   had correct parts   not close

Will Rogers Word Search

```
B O G M T C L A P U Z C Z O G E S S D
E S Z B S X G V G G I H B O T H O T B
T K Q J I R L R V V J U M H E J U B L
T A N W P O K L A H O M A I W Q Z P A
Y A F G W H M L U D I O E B N K T E C
B M Z C U N F U D G R R X P V I A U K
L H R Q B C X C E A O I U C P S S T T
A E I G O O G Y V K P S K R U E M Y U
K Q W J K I F J I B E T N X M E K Y E
E L I O M S W I L L R O G E R S M D S
Y D Q Q T C X T L L C H E R O K E E D
K G I A L I U R E L A W G B X C G K A
J I G R E A T D E P R E S S I O N K Y
H V C O L U M N I S T W H P B W L U J
U Q C H A V R S E A H D J M H H E C C
```

Word Bank

Betty Blake

Black Tuesday

Cherokee

columnist

Great Depression

humorist

Oklahoma

roper

vaudeville

Will Rogers

Will Rogers Crossword

Across

1. famous humorist and writer
3. October 29, 1929, beginning of stock market crash
4. a Native American tribe, part of Will Rogers' family history
9. ten year slump in the American economy

Down

2. 46th state in the Union, formerly an Indian Territory
5. someone who is known to be quick witted or funny
6. a variety show, from the 1880s through the 1920s
7. the woman who married Will Rogers
8. someone who writes regularly for a magazine or newspaper
10. someone skilled with a rope

Timeline

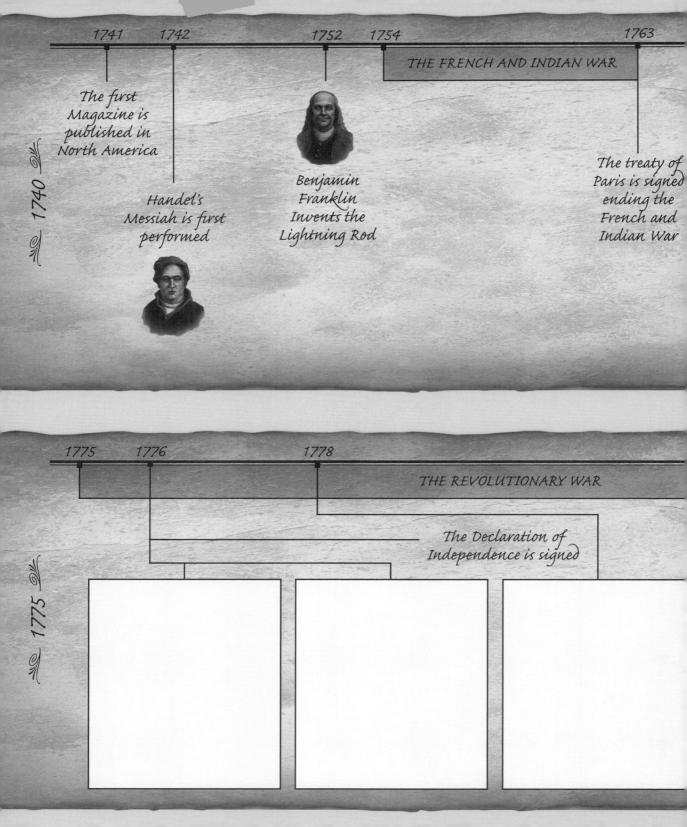

1741　1742　1752　1754　1763

THE FRENCH AND INDIAN WAR

1740

The first Magazine is published in North America

Handel's Messiah is first performed

Benjamin Franklin Invents the Lightning Rod

The treaty of Paris is signed ending the French and Indian War

1775　1776　1778

THE REVOLUTIONARY WAR

1775

The Declaration of Independence is signed

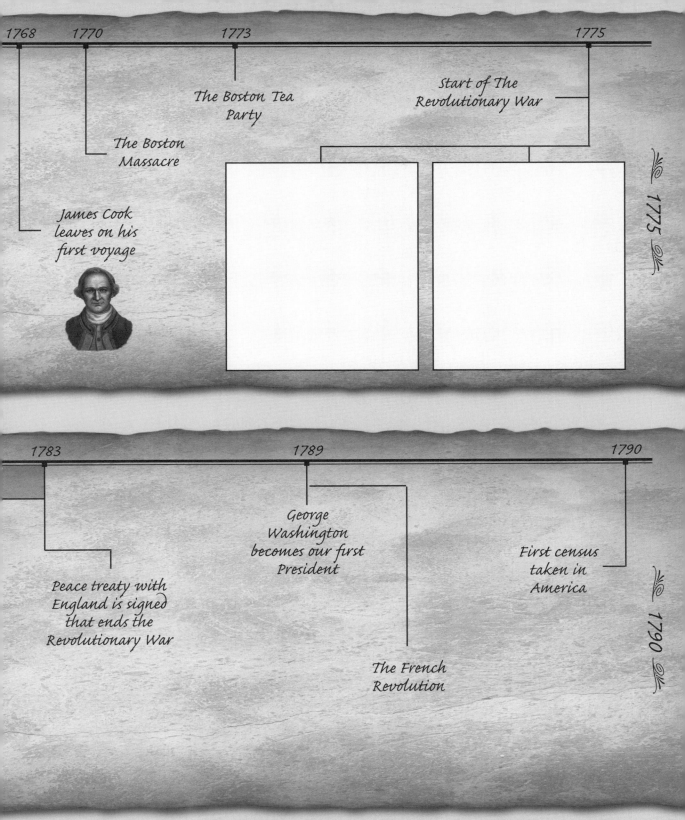

1768   1770   1773   1775

The Boston Tea
Party   Start of The
                                         Revolutionary War

The Boston
Massacre

James Cook
leaves on his
first voyage

1775

1783   1789   1790

George
Washington
becomes our first
President   First census
                                   taken in
                                   America

Peace treaty with
England is signed
that ends the
Revolutionary War

The French
Revolution

1790

1791   1794   1796   1800   1803   1804

A banking system is established in America

Thomas Jefferson becomes our 3rd president

The Louisiana Purchase

Lewis and Clark depart on the Voyage of Discovery

1790

1828   1830   1832   1836

Andrew Jackson is elected president

Abraham Lincoln begins his political career

Texas becomes an independent territory

1820

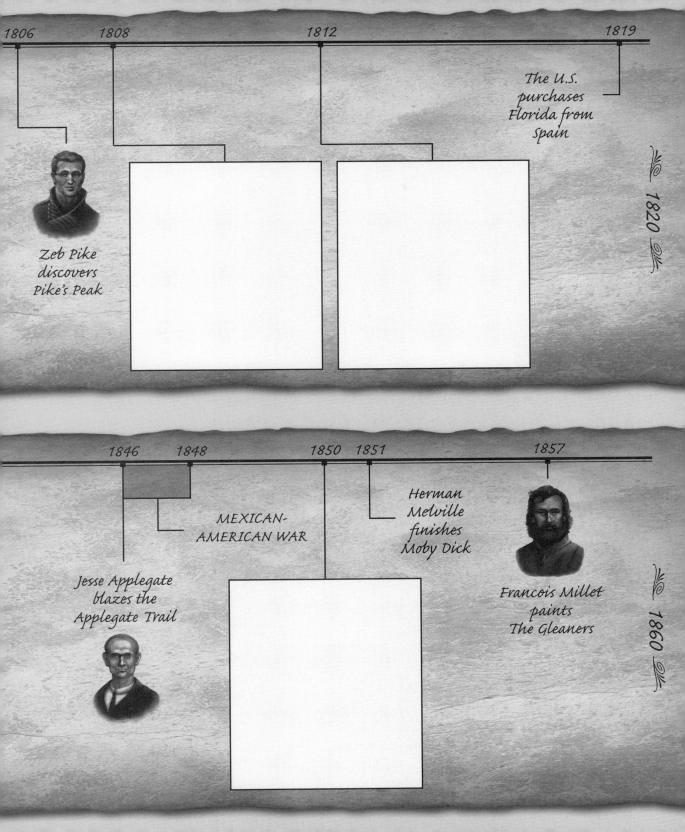

1806   1808   1812   1819

The U.S. purchases Florida from Spain

1820

Zeb Pike discovers Pike's Peak

1846   1848   1850   1851   1857

MEXICAN-AMERICAN WAR

Herman Melville finishes Moby Dick

Francois Millet paints The Gleaners

1860

Jesse Applegate blazes the Applegate Trail

1861   1862

1860

The Emancipation
Proclamation

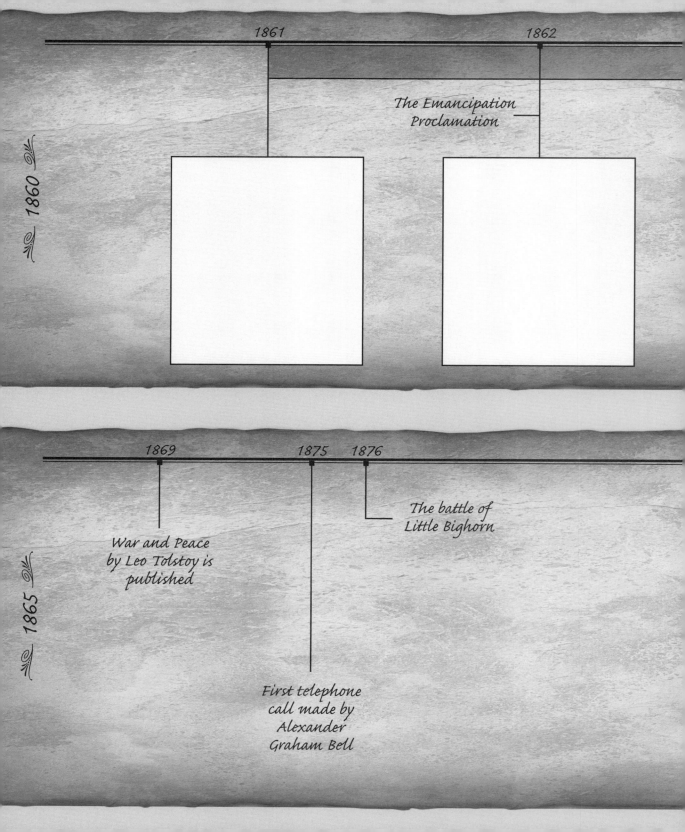

1869   1875   1876

1865

The battle of
Little Bighorn

War and Peace
by Leo Tolstoy is
published

First telephone
call made by
Alexander
Graham Bell

1863   1864   1865

THE U.S. CIVIL WAR

The 13th
Amendment is
passed

Abraham
Lincoln is
assassinated

1865

1881   1884   1885   1889

France gives the
Statue of Liberty to
the United States

The Eiffel Tower
is built

1895

1896   1903   1908   1912

The United States participates in its first Olympic Games

The first Model T built on assembly line

1895

The first successful flight by Wright brothers

1914   1917   1919   1921 1922   1927

WORLD WAR I

Albert Einstein
wins the Nobel
Prize for Physics

Charles Lindbergh
flies the first non-stop
trip across the Atlantic

America enters
World War I

1930

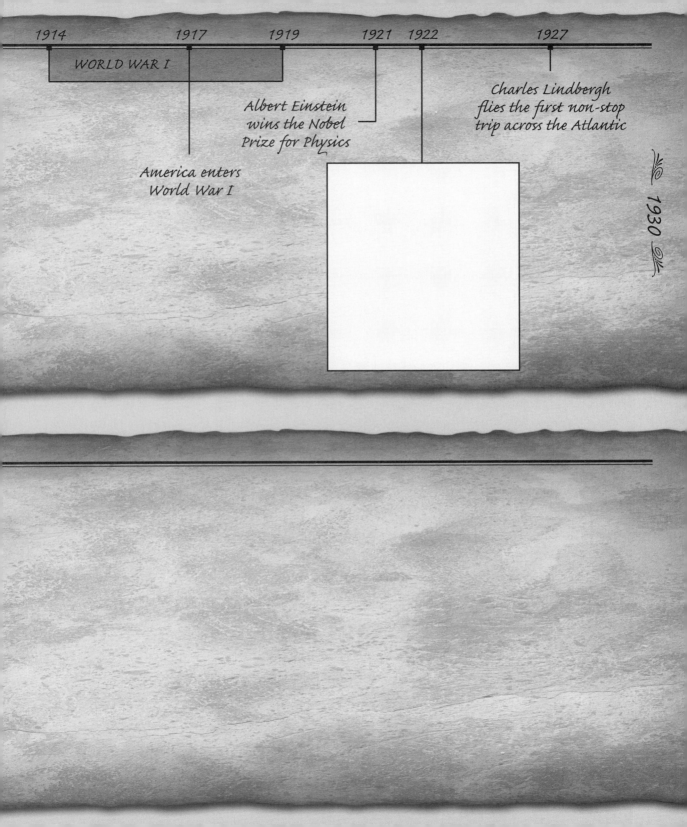

Patrick Henry
Gives most famous speech 1775

Paul Revere
Midnight Ride 1775

Thomas Paine
Common Sense is published 1776

Nathan Hale
Speaks famous last words 1776

Molly Pitcher
Battle of Monmouth 1778

Samuel Adams
Becomes Governor of MA 1794

John Adams
Becomes our 2nd President 1796

Dolley Madison
Becomes First Lady 1808

Tecumseh
Joins British forces in War 1812

Daniel Webster
"Replies to Hayne" 1830

Harriet Tubman
Helps first slaves to freedom 1850

Thomas Jackson
Becomes "Stonewall" Jackson 1861

Clara Barton
"The Angel of the Battlefield" 1862

Joshua Chamberlain
Defends Little Round Top 1863

Booker T. Washington
Opens Tuskagee Institute 1881

Samuel Clemens
Huckleberry Finn published 1884

Annie Oakley
Joins the "Wild West Show" 1885

John Philip Sousa
"The Stars and Stripes Forever" 1896

Juliette Low
First Girl Scout meeting 1912

Will Rogers
Begins career as a columnist 1922

Patrick Henry

Wordscramble:

1. Patrick Henry
2. Parsons Cause
3. orator
4. statesman
5. lawyer
6. Virginia
7. Stamp Act
8. outdoorsman
9. speech
10. parson

Before & After

1. Before
2. After
3. After
4. Before
5. After

Paul Revere

Wordscramble:

1. treason
2. Sons of Liberty
3. patriots
4. silversmith
5. Midnight Ride
6. lantern
7. Lexington
8. revolution
9. Paul Revere
10. imperative

```
X B I T G K E S B V C J T Y S L D C J
N E Z B E C H T G O R K U B B A H U W
D O R A T O R A R U B O C W W W A Z P
G Z T R I Y S T A K O Z C T N Y Q Q A
Y H Q I H D X E B K O M H H Y E T J T
F Q A P K Y Q S W S H K Z G W R B T R
G Y O S P K J M O U S T A M P A C T I
H C S P C V I A L N P H C D I J G U C
Q S T E N G P N P A R S O N W U K S K
J Z Q E Y W O U T D O O R S M A N G H
D E F C G P R I C H N G I Q N G P Z E
F L C H Y T R X O T F B E F W A S Z N
A P A R S O N S C A U S E K X S P U R
W C E M A B Q A H R V I R G I N I A Y
O A Q H D P Q Q P K P O Z L U E O G A
```

```
Q P S J O E S N I Z V T R E A S O N N
H D L O B T Q Z K P A J F R K P L G T
L T E T E F P E Z W G B U M Z T R O R
T U X S I L V E R S M I T H T F N S W
P X I R I C P B M G V G C O E Q T W V
L H N E M V C P A T R I O T S O I K K
N Z G V P A U L R E V E R E M N C Q R
E H T O E U K Q G L S T D O H A B W J
C F O L R M E F T A K C D G W A R R J
C J N U A P M I D N I G H T R I D E K
Q Z E T T H U S V T I Z Z K R N K K E
X G C I I G N P L E P V N C R U X A
A P N O V A I L C R P P F V V G I H G
M A T N E U K Q Q N R N A I G W G U E
Z C A S O N S O F L I B E R T Y X I I
```

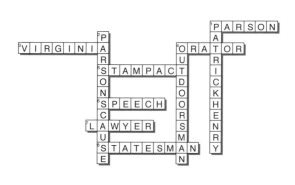

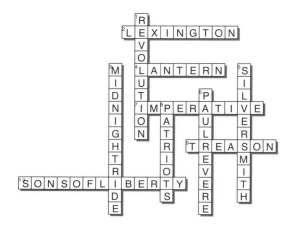

Thomas Paine

Wordscramble:

1. Thomas Paine
2. tyranny
3. pamphlet
4. Common Sense
5. The Crisis
6. Englishmen
7. The Rights of Man
8. George Washington
9. inspire
10. conviction

Nathan Hale

Wordscramble:

1. Nathan Hale
2. teacher
3. Continental Army
4. Long Island
5. Rangers
6. bravery
7. CIA
8. hero
9. volunteer
10. patriot

```
Q Y T H P N M I T D W C A P Z F Y S B
M C G P A W E O L C F O P I A D N P E
V T N N M G M C Y Q L M B F R I C B N
K V M G P Q Z I S H W M I S S U O M G
Q L T Y H H X D J M N O K S D G N D L
L X L N L Z L U N T U N I I X C V F I
X U O N E W I U G D Q S Y X N J I Q S
U Z V Y T Y R A N N Y E H W K W C L H
G E O R G E W A S H I N G T O N T T M
C J N C J J B Q C F F S P C D L I B E
V J P M D S U L E D F E V W G W O T N
P T H E C R I S I S K U K X S H N Q J
P K P T H E R I G H T S O F M A N O Q
W N I N S P I R E A C J L A N B R C U
T H O M A S P A I N E K N E S Y C K R
```

```
E Z A L V X V W H T X L L J Q N T Y X
T S J P F N Q R A T E Q H L I B R J B
I N H J V X A C M E J H P O W R G P Q
Q Y U K U Z J Y N A T H A N H A L E L
L V P R F U J T X C I A T G X V R T I
Z Q V S C B A E I H Z E R I X E N A L
T H U S U G T V J E K A I S U R U X Z
A E R L F W W I N R T G O L F Y I C I
N R A N G E R S C L A E T A D G C K Y
V O L U N T E E R I D H T N W L M R L
F G F C W V F S W Z I W D D G T D E Q
N V D C O N T I N E N T A L A R M Y Z
D H D Z V Y B S X S J Z J Q S C N T V
I P W N B W F C X S F M H A M C H Q Y
X N S V O O H O E S K F Y F Y L A L S
```

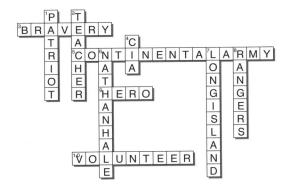

Mary Ludwig

Wordscramble:

1. Mary Ludwig Hays
2. Molly Pitcher
3. William Hays
4. cannon
5. Monmouth
6. George Washington
7. camp follower
8. heroine
9. selfless
10. brave

Before & After

1. After
2. Before
3. Before
4. After
5. Before

Samuel Adams

Wordscramble:

1. Samuel Adams
2. agitator
3. John Adams
4. Boston
5. American Revolution
6. Harvard
7. Massachusetts
8. politics
9. Boston Tea Party
10. independence

Before & After

1. Before
2. After
3. After
4. Before
5. After

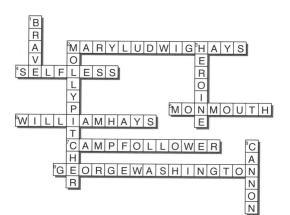

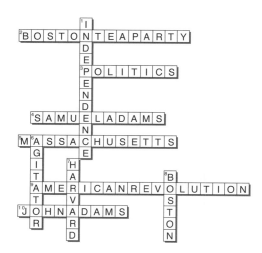

John Adams

Wordscramble:

1. John Adams
2. integrity
3. Harvard
4. conscience
5. Abigail Adams
6. John Quincy Adams
7. lawyer
8. crucial
9. Boston Massacre
10. Braintree

Dolley Madison

Wordscramble:

1. Dolley Madison
2. James Madison
3. Thomas Jefferson
4. First Lady
5. War of 1812
6. politics
7. Washington DC
8. hostess
9. Gilbert Stuart
10. Constitution

Before & After

1. Before
2. After
3. Before
4. After
5. After

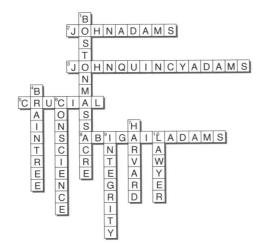

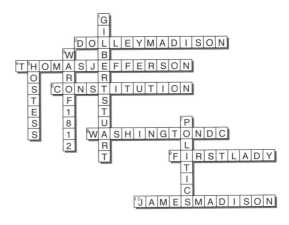

Tecumseh

Wordscramble:

1. Tecumseh
2. Shawnee
3. honor
4. barter
5. shrewd
6. charismatic
7. valiant
8. Canada
9. Proctor
10. reputation

Daniel Webster

Wordscramble:

1. Daniel Webster
2. Grace Fletcher
3. orator
4. compromise
5. Senator
6. Dartmouth
7. Constitution
8. Union
9. cherished
10. sacrifice

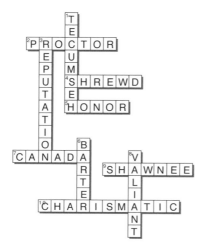

Harriet Tubman

Wordscramble:

1. abolitionist
2. Harriet Tubman
3. Underground Railroad
4. spy
5. Moses
6. Civil War
7. fugitive
8. Union Army
9. North Star
10. slavery

Before & After

1. Before
2. Before
3. After
4. Before
5. After

Thomas Jackson

Wordscramble:

1. Stonewall Brigade
2. Thomas Jackson
3. Robert E Lee
4. mortal
5. Battle of Bull Run
6. Virginia
7. West Point
8. leadership
9. loyalty
10. strategy

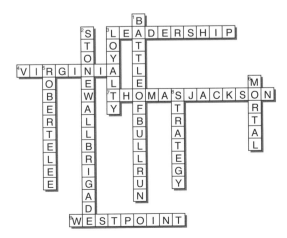

Clara Barton

Wordscramble:

1. Clara Barton
2. North Oxford
3. Battlefield Angel
4. compassion
5. mercy
6. courage
7. Union Army
8. nurse
9. Washington D C
10. optimized

Joshua Chamberlain

Wordscramble:

1. Joshua Chamberlain
2. Fannie Adams
3. Bowdoin College
4. Governor
5. professor
6. Civil War
7. Twentieth Maine
8. leader
9. honor
10. Gettysburg

Before & After

1. Before
2. After
3. After
4. Before
5. After

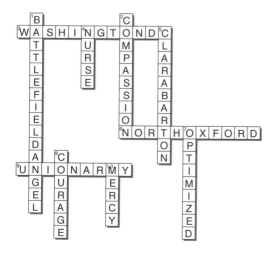

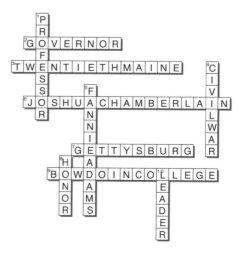

Booker T. Washington

Wordscramble:

1. Booker T Washington
2. Samuel Armstrong
3. George Washington Carver
4. negro
5. determination
6. perseverance
7. Hampton
8. Tuskegee Institute
9. legacy
10. Insatiable

Before & After

1. Before
2. After
3. After
4. After
5. Before

Samuel Clemens

Wordscramble:

1. Mark Twain
2. Samuel Clemens
3. brilliant
4. novel
5. controversial
6. Missouri
7. riverboat pilot
8. Huckleberry Finn
9. Halleys Comet
10. Ernest Hemingway

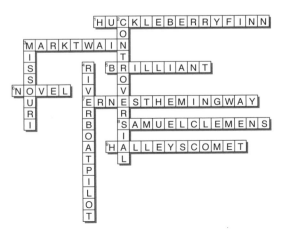

Annie Oakley

Wordscramble:

1. Annie Oakley
2. Frank Butler
3. Buffalo Bill
4. sharpshooter
5. Wild West Show
6. Darke County
7. celebrity
8. role model
9. uncompromising
10. determination

Before & After

1. Before
2. After
3. After
4. Before
5. After

John Philip Sousa

Wordscramble:

1. John Philip Sousa
2. Jane Bellis
3. Washington DC
4. Sousa Band
5. Marine Band
6. March King
7. musician
8. conductor
9. composer
10. elite

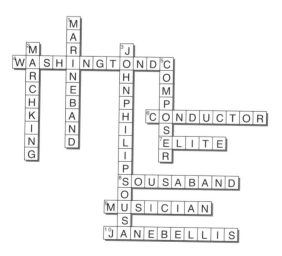

Juliette Low

Wordscramble:

1. Juliette Low
2. Robert Baden Powell
3. Girl Scouts
4. Best Scout
5. Savannah
6. courage
7. confidence
8. character
9. socialite
10. Daisy

Before & After

1. Before
2. After
3. Before
4. After
5. After

Will Rogers

Wordscramble:

1. Will Rogers
2. Betty Blake
3. roper
4. humorist
5. Cherokee
6. Oklahoma
7. Black Tuesday
8. Great Depression
9. vaudeville
10. columnis

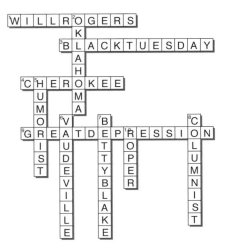

- Trail Guide to Geography Series -
by Cindy Wiggers

Three books in the *Trail Guide to ...Geography* series include U.S., World, and Bible geography. Each book provides clear directions and assignment choices to encourage self-directed learning as students create their own personal geography notebooks. Daily atlas drills, mapping activities, and various weekly assignment choices address learning styles in a way that has kids asking for more! Use each book over several years by choosing more difficult activities as students grow older.

Trail Guide features:
- Weekly lesson plans – for 36 weeks
- 5-minute daily atlas drills (2 questions/day, four days/week)
- 3 levels of difficulty – all ages participate together
- Weekly mapping assignments
- A variety of weekly research and hands-on activity choices

Student Notebooks are available on CD-ROM

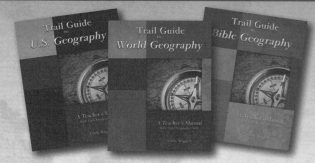

Trail Guide Levels
The *Trail Guide* Levels are just a guide. Select a level according to student ability, and match level with the appropriate atlas or student notebook.

- Primary: grades 2–4
- Intermediate: grades 5–7
- Secondary: grades 8–12
All 3 levels in each book!

Note: Primary is ideal for independent 4th graders. Second and third graders will need plenty of guidance. If your oldest is 2nd–3rd grade range, please consider *Galloping the Globe* or *Cantering the Country* first.

Trail Guide to U.S. Geography
Grades 2 - 12

"The *Trail Guide to U.S. Geography* provides lots of guidance while allowing for (and encouraging) flexibility and this is just the balance most homeschool moms need! The manual is easy to navigate and I am very impressed with how thoroughly material is covered. This resource is destined to be a favorite with homeschool families for years to come!"
–Cindy Prechtel, homeschoolingfromtheheart.com
Paperback, 144 pages, $18.95

Trail Guide to World Geography
Grades 2 - 12

"We have the *Trail Guide to World Geography* and **love** it!! We are using it again this year just for the questions... I will never sell this guide!! I am looking forward to doing the U.S. one next year."
–Shannon, OK
Paperback, 128 pages, $18.95

Trail Guide to Bible Geography
Grades 2 - 12

"Here is another winner from Geography Matters! *Trail Guide to Bible Geography* is multi-faceted, user-friendly, and suited to a wide range of ages and abilities."
–Jean Hall, Eclectic Homeschool Association
Paperback, 128 pages, $18.95

Galloping the Globe
by Loreé Pettit and Dari Mullins

Grades K - 4

"If you've got kindergarten through fourth grade students, and are looking for unit study material for geography, hold on to your hat and get ready for *Galloping the Globe!* Loreé Pettit and Dari Mullins have written this great resource to introduce children to the continents and some of their countries. This book is designed to be completed in one to three years, depending on how much time you spend on each topic. And for each continent, there are suggestions and topics galore." –Leslie Wyatt, www.homeschoolenrichment.com

Organized by continent, incorporates student notebooking, and covers these topics:

- **Basic Geography**
- **Bible**
- **History & Biographies**
- **Activities**
- **Literature**
- **Internet Sources**
- **Science**
- **Language Arts**

This new 2010 edition of *Galloping the Globe* includes an Activity CD-ROM jam-packed with all the reproducible activity sheets found in the book plus added bonus pages. Paperback with CD-ROM, 272 pages, $29.95

Cantering the Country
by Loreé Pettit and Dari Mullins

Grades 1–5

Saddle up your horses and strap on your thinking caps. Learning geography is an adventure. From the authors who brought you *Galloping the Globe,* you'll love its U.S. counterpart, *Cantering the Country*. This unit study teaches a wide range of academic and spiritual disciplines using the geography of the U.S. as a starting point. With this course, you won't have to put aside one subject to make time for another. They're all connected! This comprehensive unit study takes up to three years to complete and includes all subjects except math and spelling. Incorporates student notebooking and covers these topics:

- **U.S. Geography**
- **Activities**
- **Character**
- **Literature**
- **Science**
- **Civics**
- **Language Arts**
- **History & Biographies & More**

In addition to the 250+ page book, you will receive a CD-ROM packed full of reproducible outline maps and activities. Dust off your atlas and get ready to explore America! Paperback with CD-ROM, 272 pages, $29.95

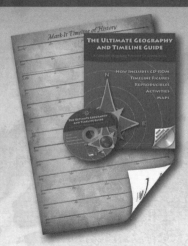

The Ultimate Geography and Timeline Guide
by Maggie Hogan and Cindy Wiggers

Grades K - 12

Learn how to construct timelines, establish student notebooks, teach geography through literature, and integrate science with activities on volcanoes, archaeology, and other subjects. Use the complete multi-level geography course for middle and high school students. Now includes CD-ROM of all reproducible activity and planning pages. Use for all students kindergarden through high school. Paperback with CD-ROM, 353 pages, $39.95

- 18 Reproducible Outline Maps
- Teaching Tips
- Planning Charts
- Over 150 Reproducible Pages
- Over 300 Timeline Figures
- Lesson Plans
- Scope and Sequence
- Flash Cards
- Games

Mark-It Timeline of History
There's hardly no better way to keep history in perspective than creating a timeline in tandem with your history studies. This poster is just the tool to do so. Write or draw images of events as they are studied, or attach timeline figures to aid student understanding and comprehension of the topic at hand. 23" x 34". Laminated, $10.95, Paper (folded), $5.95

Adventures of Munford Series
by Jamie Aramini

Although he's just two parts hydrogen and one part oxygen, Munford is all adventure. He can be rain, snow, sleet, or steam. He has traveled the world in search of excitement. Throughout history, he has been present at some of the most important and world-changing events. Fun and educational, Munford will inspire your children to learn more about many of history's greatest events. These readers make a great addition to your learning experience in areas such as history, geography, and science. This book series was written on an elementary reading level, but provides plenty of read-aloud entertainment for the entire family! Paperback, $8.95

The American Revolution

In this adventure, Munford travels to colonial America and experiences first hand the events leading to the American Revolution. He meets famed American Founding Fathers, such as Samuel Adams, Thomas Jefferson, and George Washington. He joins the Sons of Liberty under cover of night to dump tea into Boston Harbor. He tags along for Paul Revere's most famous ride, and even becomes a part of the Declaration of Independence in a way that you might not expect!

The Klondike Gold Rush

In this adventure, Munford finds himself slap into the middle of the Klondike Gold Rush. He catches gold fever on this dangerous, yet thrilling, adventure. Meet some of the Gold Rush's most famous characters, like gold baron Alex McDonald or the tricky villain named Soapy Smith. Take a ride on the Whitehorse Rapids, and help Munford as he pans for gold. This is an adventure you won't soon forget!

Munford Meets Lewis & Clark

Join Munford on an epic adventure with Meriwether Lewis and William Clark, as they make their perilous journey in search of the Northwest Passage to the Pacific Ocean.

... More to Come!

Look for more adventures in this exciting series as Munford's journey through time and territory continues around the world.

Eat Your Way Through the USA
by Loreé Pettit

Taste your way around the U.S.A. without leaving your own dining room table! Each state has its unique geographical features, culinary specialities, and agricultural products. These influence both the ingredients that go into a recipe and the way food is prepared. Compliment your geography lesson and tantalize your tastebuds at the same time with this outstanding cookbook.

This cookbook includes a full meal of easy to follow recipes from each state. Recipes are easy to follow. Though they aren't written at a child's level, it's easy to include your students in the preparation of these dishes. Cooking together provides life skills and is a source of bonding and pride. More than just a cookbook, it is a taste buds-on approach to geography. Spiral bound, 118 pages, $14.95

Eat Your Way Around the World
by Jamie Aramini

Get out the sombrero for your Mexican fiesta! Chinese egg rolls... corn pancakes from Venezuela...fried plantains from Nigeria. All this, and more, is yours when you take your family on a whirlwind tour of over thirty countries in this unique international cookbook. Includes a full meal of recipes from each country. Recipes are easy to follow, and ingredients are readily available. Jam-packed with delicious dinners, divine drinks, and delectable desserts, this book is sure to please.

The entire family will be fascinated with tidbits of culture provided for each country including: Etiquette hints, Food Profiles, and Culture a la Carté. For more zest, add an activity and violà, create a memorable learning experience that will last for years to come. Some activities include: Food Journal, Passport, and World Travel Night. Spiral bound, 120 pages, $14.95

Geography Through Art
by Sharon Jeffus and Jamie Aramini

Geography Through Art is the ultimate book of international art projects. Join your children on an artistic journey to more than twenty-five countries spanning six continents (includes over a dozen United States projects). Previously published by Visual Manna as *Teaching Geography Through Art*, Geography Matters has added a number of enhancements and practical changes to this fascinating art book. Use this book as an exciting way to supplement any study of geography, history, or social studies. You'll find yourself reaching for this indispensable guide again and again to delight and engage students in learning about geography through the culture and art of peoples around the world. Paperback, 190 pages, $19.95

Lewis & Clark - Hands On
Art and English Activities
by Sharon Jeffus

Follow the experiences of Meriwether Lewis and William Clark with hands on art and writing projects associated with journal entries made during the Corps of Discovery Expedition. Ideal for adding interest to any Lewis and Clark study or to teach drawing and journaling. Includes profiles of American artists, step by step drawing instructions, actual journal entries, and background information about this famous adventure. Paperback, 80 pages, $12.95

Profiles from History - Volume 1
by Ashley (Strayer) Wiggers

When studying history, a human connection is the most important connection that we can make. In *Profiles from History*, your student will not only learn about twenty famous people – but also why each one is worthy of remembrance. Everyone knows that Benjamin Franklin was a great inventor, but how many realize he was also a great man? He valued helping people more than making money or becoming famous. He refused to patent his popular Franklin stove, so more families could keep their homes warm during the cold, winter months. *Profiles from History* tells stories like this one, stories of greatness and inspiration. Each profile includes fun activities such as crosswords, word search, & timeline usage. Paperback, $16.95   Also availible: *Profiles from History - Volume 2*. Paperback, $16.95

- Reproducible Outline Maps -

Reproducible outline maps have a myriad of uses in the home, school, and office. Uncle Josh's quality digital maps provide opportunities for creative learning at all ages. His maps feature rivers and grid lines where possible, and countries are shown in context with their surroundings. (No map of Germany "floating" in the center of the page, here!) When students use outline maps and see the places they are studying in context they gain a deeper understanding of the subject at hand.

Uncle Josh's Outline Map Book

Take advantage of those spontaneous teaching moments when you have this set of outline maps handy. They are:

• Over 100 reproducible maps
• 15 world regions
• Continents with and without borders
• 25 countries
• Each of the 50 United States
• 8 U.S. regions

Useful for all grades and topics, this is by far one of the best book of reproducible outline maps you'll find. Paperback, 128 pages, $19.95

Uncle Josh's Outline Map Collection CD-ROM

In addition to all maps in *Uncle Josh's Outline Map Book* the CD-Rom includes color, shaded-relief, and labeled maps. Over 260 printable maps plus bonus activities. CD-ROM (Mac & Windows), $26.95

- Large-scale Maps -

Large-scale maps are great for detail labeling and for family or classroom use. Laminated Mark-It maps can be reused for a variety of lessons. Quality digital map art is used for each of the fifteen map titles published and laminated by Geography Matters. Choose from large scale continents, regions, United States, and world maps. US and World available in both outline version and with state, country, and capitals labeled. Ask about our ever expanding library of full, color shaded-relief maps. Paper and laminated, each title available separately or in discounted sets.

TRAIL GUIDE TO LEARNING

Introducing… *The Trail Guide to Learning series*, an innovative new curriculum from Geography Matters. This series provides all the guidance and materials necessary to teach your children the way you've always wanted—effectively, efficiently, and enjoyably. But most of all, *Trail Guide to Learning* equips you to achieve the foremost objective of a homeschooling program—developing and nurturing relationships with your children! The tutoring approach makes each lesson individual, yet flexible enough to meet the needs of several grades at once. The sourcebook provides the instruction, clearly laid out in daily sections that make lesson planning a breeze. Just add in the necessary resources for success, available in our money-saving packages, and you'll have a curriculum for multiple grade levels that will last all year and cover every subject but math!

Paths of Exploration
Grades 3-5

Paths of Settlement
Grades 4-6

Paths of Exploration takes students on a journey. Follow the steps of famous explorers and pioneers across America and let geography be your guide to science, history, language skills, and the arts. This journey will teach students HOW to think by asking, answering, and investigating questions about our great country's beginning and growth. The paths of the explorers are seen through multidisciplinary eyes, but always with the same goals: to make learning enjoyable, memorable, and motivating. This full one-year course for 3rd, 4th and 5th graders (adaptable for 2nd and 6th) covers six units in two volumes.

Walk the *Paths of Settlement* with famous Americans such as George Washington, Patrick Henry, John and Abigail Adams, Francis Scott Key, Clara Barton, Robert E. Lee, Abraham Lincoln, Laura Ingalls Wilder and Booker T. Washington. They built upon the trail blazed by brave explorers and their actions teach us the principles of freedom and citizenship founding and expanding our country, strengthening us in times of war and binding us together in times of struggle.

Paths of Progress
Grades 5-7

Your children will take a tour of America, yesterday and today, learning about geography, geology, and weather along the way! Multimedia makes music and history come to life, while literature, art and activities beautifully illustrate the times. Language skills are included equipping your children to express their thoughts and reflect their learning naturally.

Look online now for more information and to view sample pages.

www.TrailGuidetoLearning.com • **800-426-4650**

About the Author

Ashley M. Wiggers grew up in the early days of the home schooling movement taught by parents, Greg and Debbie Strayer, who are authors of numerous home schooling materials. Ashley recently retired from a 10-year career as a national champion synchronized swimmer, is a swim instructor at the YMCA, and coaches the Pulaski County High School swim team. She also speaks at home school seminars across the country, edits a monthly online newsletter for Geography Matters, and has written the *Profiles from History* Series. Ashley makes her home in Somerset, KY, with her husband, Alex.